A SaipanLiving.com Survival Guide

Doing Business On Saipan!

A step-by-step survival guide for finding opportunity, launching a business and profiting in the US Commonwealth of the Northern Mariana Islands of Saipan, Tinian and Rota

Walt F.J. Goodridge
Author of *Turn Your Passion Into Profit*
& founder of SaipanLiving.com & WeLoveSaipan.com

Doing Business on Saipan!

Published by The Passion Profit Company, an imprint of
a company called W, New York
P.O. Box 618
Church Street Station
New York, NY 10008-0618

Distributed exclusively by
The Passion Profit Company
www.PassionProfit.com
orders@passionprofit.com
Order online at
www.SaipanLiving.com

Retail Cost: $19.95
ISBN-10: 0-9745313-5-9
ISBN-13: 978-0-9745313-5-9

First Edition: February 2010

Disclaimer:

This guide is NOT written by the department of tourism. It was written by the entrepreneur founder of SaipanLiving.com. The goal is to provide you with information, inspiration and ideas you can use to first arrive at a decision as to whether to do business on Saipan, and then, what type of business venture you wish to embark on.

Breaking News! Federalization, Immigration and Labor Update

View the latest updates to this page at www.destinationsaipan.com

On November 28, 2009, the U.S. Commonwealth of the Northern Mariana Islands (CNMI), which includes the islands of Saipan, Tinian and Rota, came under United States Federal Immigration and Labor laws. This was as a result of Public Law 110-229 (The Consolidated Natural Resources Act of 2008). This new law and the resulting regulations will affect tourism to, life on and doing business on Saipan. Certain aspects of previous CNMI law will be extended during the 2-year transition period until November 28, 2011. As of this writing, here are some of the relevant points that affect doing business on Saipan:

- **Russian and Chinese Visa Waiver**

After November 28, 2009, Russian and Chinese tourists will still be able to visit Saipan without need of a visa.

- **Umbrella Permit for non-resident contract workers**

All 13,000 non-resident workers ("contract workers" "guest workers") on Saipan, Tinian and Rota will be granted an "umbrella permit" which will allow continued residency in the CNMI for the next two years after federalization of the immigration laws. This permit and related decisions at this critical moment of immigration changes within the CNMI should be closely followed by anyone interested in doing business on Saipan.

- **Minimum Wage**

The next scheduled increase in the minimum wage will be from $4.50/hour to $5.00/hour and will occur on July 25, 2010.

How to Use this Guide

It may seem somewhat unnecessary to give instructions on how to read what appears to be a very straightforward guide. However, here are a few tips on gaining the most from this manual which may be applied to any new venture.

1. Never go past a word or phrase you don't understand. It's been proven that the only reason people give up on a new project or course of study is because they encounter a word, phrase or concept for which they have no definition, or the wrong definition. I've made an effort to explain words or terms that may be new to you and your understanding of Saipan, and there is a glossary in the Appendix. If a word in this guide is new to you, please take the time to use a dictionary or the Internet to find the most appropriate meaning. This tip is more important than most people know!

2. ☑ Use the checkboxes. The purpose of this guide is to help you take the necessary actions to do business on Saipan. To help you keep track of the specific steps that apply to your business, I've provided checkboxes next to tax requirements, forms, applications, permits and other action steps. Not all the checkboxes will apply to your specific business. If you are reading the ebook version, you are

3. Read this guide at least twice. I encourage you to read through the guide once to get a general overview, and then read through again to take notes.

Key:

Items with a superscript of "1" (e.g. CNMI[1]) the first time they appear, are defined in the Glossary, located in the back of this guide.

Table of Contents

Why I Wrote This Book

This book was created to be the answer to the following email:

Dear Walt,

I'd like to thank you for the articles you continue to write for the Saipan Tribune. I hope you don't mind my frankness, but at first, I did not read them, as they were too "self-helpish" in their content. However, your persistence in communicating the message of taking control of your situation, started to stick and pique my curiosity, until finally I started reading your columns.

Anyway, you've done a great job in stirring the entrepreneurial spirit in me, and with others in the community. I'm going through the process of figuring out what I can offer to the community as my passion and hopefully it could lead to me putting a product out there soon, and hopefully one day surpassing what my day job could ever offer.

In this process though, what I find challenging is maneuvering through the "startup" effort and what resources are out there. Getting to that idea and the leap of faith, the surpassing of one's fear to just go for it, is what you've been great at, but what would also be great is to line up the information for someone to take it to the next level. For example, how should you organize yourself? For instance, if you chose sole proprietorship, you just go to Rev & Tax and get a business license, but what if you want to incorporate or do an LLC? Well, then you need to work with an attorney, or if you have the moxy (or can't afford an attorney), organize yourself and get registered at the Department of Commerce. Once you've got your license, you need to open a business bank account, and banks require, this, this and this, as an example.

I guess in a roundabout way, a resource guide on setting up your own business in the CNMI is what's needed. Anyhow, hmm, maybe I can put this together (ack, another idea). Or maybe a round table of business folks to query, or maybe a mentor program. Resources such as these would be great to close the loop on one's idea, one's passion, so that when one gets their head out of the clouds and rainbows, determined to do something about their dream, they can get onto the ground with pointers on things that they need to be aware of when one ventures out as a new business.

Keep up the inspiration. I hope this feedback makes sense and thanks for being open to receive it. Cheers, --Xavier Castro

Thanks, Xavier. And special thanks also to:

- Joe Hill, lawyer and long time Saipan resident
- Tony Pellegrino, business owner
- Pam Halstead, Business License Officer, Dept of Finance
- Senator Maria Pangelinan
- Oscar Camacho, Commonwealth Development Authority

I now present: *Doing Business on Saipan!*

Introduction:
The Truth About Saipan

If you're like me, a title like "The Truth About [anything]" is a compelling one that makes you want to read more. I believe we all, on some level, yearn to know the truth. Especially if you've heard contrasting things about life on Saipan, it would be nice, once and for all, to get to the truth of it all, wouldn't it?

The truth is, however, there *is* no single truth about Saipan. In any attempt to uncover the truth, what we find are subjective perspectives, opinions and observations determined by individual agendas. Some agendas are simple: *(eg. "I want to make everyone as miserable as I am").* Some agendas are complex. (*eg. "We will organize a federal takeover, reshape it in our image, and make this an R&R [rest and relaxation] spot for the troops.")*

Even the news media has an agenda. People joke that the media's motto is *"Never let the truth get in the way of a good story!"* A good (i.e. salacious) story sells papers, magazines and advertising. Yes, the truth changes based on who is speaking and what they want out of life.

So, whether Saipan is a "Pacific paradise" or a "den of corruption" is all based on one's perspective and agenda. If you are a pessimist who wants people to wallow in your misery, then Saipan is one thing. If you're an optimist, bent on helping improve conditions, it's another. If you call yourself a "realist" (generally a pessimist in disguise), then things generally tend toward the negative with the disclaimer that you're just being real.

But that's all okay, because if you know a person's agenda, then everything they say and do makes sense (unless their agenda is specifically to confuse you about what their agenda is; or unless they're just crazy). And, if you know a person's agenda, then you won't be unduly misled by their claims to truth.

Walt's Agenda

So, with that said, what's MY agenda? As the author of several passionpreneur[1] books, and as evidenced by the title of my weekly column [The Saipanpreneur Project], my agenda is to encourage people to start their own businesses based on their passions. However, I have other agendas as well. One is to help all peoples optimize their assets, achieve empowerment, and maintain control over the things that matter to them. Here on Saipan--for my own selfish reasons--I'd like to maintain the cultural diversity, natural beauty, and uncomplicated lifestyle that I've come to love about living here.

But wait, there's more. There's also a part of my agenda that some may consider subversive, and that is to reveal the underlying deception of most modern ideals and belief systems, encourage a lifestyle that values simplicity and minimalism instead of consumerism, and excess, one that favors the natural over the artificial, and at the same time that honors everyone's right and freedom to choose whichever lifestyle works for them.

My goal is to help people arrive at a set of choices that creates a clean environment, promotes optimal health, safeguards the rights and freedoms of all, and offers an effective understanding of reality.

Every column I write, every website I launch, and every project I embark upon includes a combination of some or all of those agendas. But don't be misled. Remember my agenda. It's not my nature to focus on the negative, however "real" the realists say it is. People who harp on doom won't start businesses or see the opportunity in the "doom."

Even <u>my</u> facts are selectively offered based on my agenda and what I want you to see. Even though I strive for a 50-50 balance, I'll always tend to give at least 51 percent (accentuate the positive, and eliminate the negative, as Bing Crosby sang) to aid the possibility of victory and the triumph of hope.

The Truth About Saipan

So, with that said, here is my truth about Saipan:

* Saipan is overcoming a branding challenge. In other words, what comes to mind when people think of "Saipan" isn't always what those of us who actually live and work here think are its best assets. We're emerging from the shadow of an era tainted by a controversial garment industry, and bad (accurate or not) press.

* Like the rest of the world, there's an economic transition taking place on Saipan. In addition, there are agendas for federalization[1], as well as immigration and labor reform, which make this an island on the verge. However, even with these and other changes and challenges, there are a multitude of assets which make this a great place to visit, vacation, live, learn and love!

* Great Weather: Saipan holds the Guinness World Record for most consistent temperature. The average difference between night and day is greater than the average difference between winter and summer.

* Natural beauty: There is natural, pristine beauty here: beautiful sunrises, beaches, foliage, fruits, sunsets, rock formations, aquatic life and more!

* Proximity to Marianas Trench[1] (the deepest part of the world's oceans): While no one actually goes diving that deep, our proximity to such a rich, bio-diverse, unexplored region of the world's oceans has blessed us with underwater life that makes Saipan one of the best places for…

* World class diving: World class shore diving, "Eagle Ray City," and the Grotto are just some of the activities and locations Saipan divers rave about.

* Discovery of ecological significance: Scientists and students of ecology can learn much about life on our planet from our coral reefs (estimated value comparable to Hawaii's), and the pristine, biodiversity of our waters. The U.S. government recently created the Marianas Trench Marine National Monument[1] (an area of over 12,000 square nautical miles) in recognition of this significance.

* Cultural diversity: Life on Saipan has been influenced by the Spanish, Germans, Japanese, and Americans! The presence of indigenous Chamorro[1] and Carolinian[1] people, immigrants, guest workers, tourists, investors and students from Asia, the Pacific, and America, make this a place of unprecedented cultural/ethnic potential.

* Historical significance: Saipan was a key battle site during World War II. It's been said the Cold War[1] started on Tinian, the island just 3 miles south of Saipan! That's where the atomic bombs dropped on Japan were launched!

* Archeological significance: Ancient artifacts of some of the planet's earliest civilizations are found here.

* Unsolved mysteries: The case could be made that there are stories waiting to be told about the Amelia Earhart[1] mystery, sunken Spanish treasure ships, World War II disappearances, ancient civilizations in which Saipan figures prominently. What might you discover on your own?

And that's just *some* of the truth about Saipan. (Don't forget my agenda). Despite its challenges, many who come, stay. Many who leave miss it terribly. And many who travel the world over come back to enjoy a way of life they can't find anywhere else. Those of us who actually live and work on Saipan know this to be truth.

'Come See For Yourself!'

Ultimately, the only way to discover the truth about Saipan is to come see for yourself! But it would be wise to heed the moral of this story:

Once upon a time, a person moved into a new town and asked one of the town residents, "What are the people in this town like?"

"What were the people like in the town you just left?" the resident asked in return.

The new person answered, "They were unfriendly and nasty."

And the town resident said, "I think you'll find the people here are just about the same."

Later, the same resident was approached by another new arrival, who asked the same question. Again, the resident asked, "What were the people like in the town you just left?"

The answer was "The people were warm and friendly." And the resident answered, "I think you'll find the people here are just about the same."

Saipan Living Invitation

As founder of SaipanLiving.com, I receive questions and inquiries every day from people who are considering moving to Saipan to live, work, start businesses, rent property, escape the rat race, or simply live a different lifestyle. If you'd like to share your truth with them, as the content on the site is being developed, please visit www.saipanliving.com and/or email me to become an expert and answer their questions. I encourage you to participate, otherwise their perception of Saipan will be "the world according to Walt," (and who wants a bunch of subversive, minimalist, Jamaican, vegan idealists running around island?)

P.S. On the site, you'll also discover some interesting truths about the little-known Touwlawos[1] people of Saipan! I think you'll find them interesting.

So there you have it. Saipan's past and present. Welcome to the future. Prepare yourself for the New Saipan!

--Walt Goodridge
Founder of SaipanLiving.com

Chapter 1: THE CASE FOR SAIPAN

Can I make money on Saipan???

That's the bottom line. It's essentially what everyone is asking, and presumably why you are reading this book. The answer, as you can imagine, is not an easy one. Ultimately, you will have to answer it for yourself. However, what I *can* offer you are facts, figures, feelings, opinions, observations, and overviews, historical perspectives, polls and a personal passion that you can use to compile all the information you require. What I *will* tell you however, from a look at history, as well as my own personal experience, is that even in the US Great Depression of the 1930s, some people were able to amass great fortunes. Secondly, it's always the case that *"One man's trash is another man's treasure."* By that, I mean simply that there is opportunity everywhere for those who can see it. My answer, therefore, is the same on Saipan as it is everywhere:

1. if you can generate business from a wider geography, and

2. if you can incorporate some internet component to your business so you're not solely reliant on the local economy, and

3. if you can anticipate the "new needs" given the current situation and changing paradigm,

then, you might be able to position yourself to ride out the storm, and be ahead of the pack when things settle and start to turn around. We'll explore these survival concepts in more detail in a later section. With that said, let's take a closer look at what's happening on Saipan.

A Pivotal Time: 8 Factors Affecting Saipan

Doing Business on Saipan is being published at a pivotal time in Saipan's history. There are many factors that are, and that will continue to affect the economic climate, the mood and opportunities on Saipan. These eight, however, are arguably the most significant at this time:

1. Federalization
2. Increase in minimum wage
3. Effects of the garment industry departure
4. Tourism
5. The "military buildup" on neighboring Guam[1]
6. Global economic downturn
7. CNMI Zoning Law
8. Article 12

1. Federalization

For most of its relationship with the United States, the CNMI administered its own immigration and labor laws. Starting in 2008, Saipan's labor laws were set on a course to catch up to federal standards. Federalization of Saipan's immigration is scheduled to take effect on November 28, 2009. At that time, visa requirements, entry and exit requirements, status of contract workers as well as their immediate relatives will all be affected.

2. Increase in Minimum Wage

One specific aspect of federalization that has had a tremendous effect on doing business on Saipan has been the increase in the minimum wage. For 11 years, the minimum hourly wage for contract workers on Saipan was fixed at $3.05/hour. On July 24, 2007, the first 50-cent increase occurred. The wage is scheduled to increase by $0.50 every year to finally be consistent with the national minimum wage of $7.25 by 2015.

3. The Departure of the Garment Industry

In January of 2009, the last garment factory on Saipan closed its doors. Many factories moved their operations to other countries like Vietnam in order to find more profitable economic conditions. Many cite low profitability as a result of the lifting of trade quotas (which increased imports from competing countries), as well as increasing costs due to the rising minimum wage.

4. Tourism

Tourism, which has been touted as Saipan's one remaining major industry, and which has brought visitors primarily from Asian countries (Japan, Korea, China) as well as Russia, is experiencing a downturn as a result of many factors including a slowed global economy and pandemic[1] (i.e. swine flu) fears.

5. The Military Buildup

It's been known for quite some time that US military personnel, currently stationed on Okinawa, will be redeployed to Guam and Tinian. Some people see this as a good thing that will result in increased numbers of residents, construction contracts, and a better standard of living. Others see this as more of the "federalization," "takeover" and militarization of the region which will result in loss of self-rule, culture and identity.

6. Global Economic Downturn

Of course, all of this is happening amid what many are calling the worst economic downturn since the Great Depression of 1939. Saipan is not immune to the effects of the global economy. However, it is safe to say—and this is important for anyone doing business on Saipan—that because of Saipan's unique geographical location, as well as its cultural background and traditional business relationships, its economy cannot be adequately predicted by a solely US or solely Asian perspective. Many argue that the CNMI is more closely linked to what's happening in Asia, rather than the US.

7. CNMI Zoning Law

In 2007, new zoning regulations were passed. These laws affect where and what types of businesses can be operated on the island. Anyone seeking to do business on Saipan must be approved and zoned correctly.

8. Article 12

When people here on Saipan talk about "Article 12," they are referring to the section of the CNMI Constitution which limits purchase and ownership of land in the CNMI to people of Northern Marianas descent. Anyone else can, however, sign a 55-year lease for property on which to do business.

Section 805 of the Covenant allows the CNMI to revisit this "land alienation restriction" 25 years after the termination of the Trusteeship Agreement which ended in 1986. Therefore, in 2011, Article 12 will be up for reconsideration and possible constitutional amendment possibly by a constitutional convention of elected delegates, a popular initiative, or a legislative initiative.

Those in favor of repealing (ending) Article 12 cite that investors will not invest in the CNMI because they cannot own the land. Allowing foreign investors to purchase land will increase investment in the island. They say that it will allow local owners to benefit from doing what they see fit to do with their property.

Those in favor of keeping things as they are fear that eventually the indigenous population will be pushed off their land as property values rise, property taxes increase, and foreign interests privatize access to land. An insightful article in favor of keeping things as they are, and of being cautious about repealing Article 12 appeared in the Saipan Tribune March 28, 2008. It was written by Brad Doerr and is entitled "The Great Saipan Land Rush….Not!"

Putting it all Together

All these factors have resulted in:

- Business closures as once-profitable businesses cease operations.
- Changing population numbers as residents leave for perceived greener pastures in Guam.
- Changing demographics as guest workers return to China, Thailand, the Philippines, Korea, Japan, Bangladesh and neighboring islands.
- Lower sales in some industries.
- Vacant homes and apartments.

This is a land in transition.

Ready for the *good* news?

The good news is:

This is a land in transition.

As a result, there is opportunity for those who choose to see it.

Advantages of Doing Business on Saipan

Jones Act Exemption

[*Wikipedia*] "The **Merchant Marine Act of 1920** (P.L. 66-261) *is a United States Federal statute that regulates maritime commerce in U.S. waters and between U.S. ports. Section 27, also known as the Jones Act, deals with cabotage (i.e., coastal shipping) and requires that all goods transported by water between U.S. ports be carried in U.S.-flag ships, constructed in the United States, owned by U.S. citizens, and crewed wholly by U.S. citizens. The purpose of the law is to support the U.S. merchant marine industry. People who oppose the Jones Act say that requiring that goods be transported on US-flag ships raises the cost of shipping.*

"*There are certain American ports which are exempt from provisions of the Jones Act. They are Guam, American Samoa and the Northern Marianas in the Pacific and the United States Virgin Islands in the Caribbean.*"

What this means is that shipping costs to and from Saipan could be more competitive as goods can be shipped on vessels

Pending Free Trade Zone

While not yet executed, Public Law 12-20 or the Free Trade Zone Act has been passed. The Free Trade Zone Act seeks to stimulate the local economy through the creation of free trade zones, the creation of tax incentives, and the establishment of a public corporation to administer free trade zones.

The US Postal System

Even though "Saipan," the "CNMI," "Northern Mariana Islands" or "NMI" are not household names on the mainland, (many –even government--websites, forms and applications don't list us as a state option or part of the US), we here on Saipan have a unique advantage.

The CNMI is, in fact, part of the United States and is, therefore, served by the United States Postal System (USPS). This allows domestic as well as foreign businesses based on Saipan full access to the entire US population plus the rest of the world through an efficient delivery system at the same postal rates as their mainland counterparts. In other words, you can send a letter from Saipan to Bayonne, New Jersey at the same first class postage rate as if you were sending it from Brooklyn, New York.

As the owner of a mail order business, my own decision to move to Saipan was greatly influenced by this advantage. I was able to maintain a cost-effective connection to my (mostly US) customers even while basking in the Saipan sun!

And while we're on the subject of shipping, Federal Express, DHL and UPS all have offices here on Saipan.

Strategic Location and proximity to Asian Markets

Saipan is quite unique in that it is a piece of America uniquely situated in a predominantly Asian market. Saipan's economy is affected more directly by consumer moods, speculation and fluctuations from the Asian continent. This can allow US-based companies to reach Asian consumers, and can allow Asian companies access to US consumers.

Summary of Even More Advantages

Living in the Marianas, one experiences a year-round summer climate with all of the sophisticated amenities of a tourist resort area, yet with a "small town" atmosphere, traditional family values, and friendly neighbors. To do business here means working in a multi-cultural community of local and international businesses.

With the beautiful, unspoiled environment as the key attraction, tourism has been the primary force that has developed the Northern Marianas. However, a wide range of other business opportunities exist in these islands. A few of the significant investment incentives and advantages for businesses includes:

- The protection of American judicial system and U.S. laws including those that relate to copyright, trademark, patent regulations and the protection of intellectual property;
- Trading in U.S. dollar currency, with no restrictions on repatriation of profits or capital;
- Significant tax advantages for executives and all employees on Northern Marianas sourced income;

- Ports that are free of United States Customs duties,
- Duty free status for certain eligible goods to be exported to the US;
- Favorable tariff treatment for qualified exports to other countries;
- Reliable, scheduled ocean shipping and exemption from the Federal "Jones Act," which allows foreign flag vessels to enter CNMI ports;
- Exemption from U.S. vessel documentation laws for companies licensed in the Northern Marianas;
- State-of-the-art telecommunications linked by undersea fiber optic cable to worldwide facilities.

Challenges of Doing Business on Saipan

Weak Infrastructure

It's no secret that certain roads, sewer lines, power lines, utilities on Saipan are in need of repair.

Rising Shipping/Fuel Costs

When the garment factories left Saipan, the effects reached far beyond simply the loss of job opportunities for contract workers. Specifically, when the factories were operating at their prime, there were shipments of containers of clothing leaving the island. Shipping companies could make money bringing containers of goods into the CNMI, and make money taking containers out. However, as the factories closed, the number of outgoing shipments dwindled, and, so the shipping companies made less money on exports, but still had the same expenses bringing containers to the island. To make up for this loss in revenue, as fuel costs increased, they have had to raise prices. Therefore, it costs more much more money these days to ship containers to the island.

Power Crisis

Oil price increases and high costs associated with power production have also been compounded by infrastructure challenges. The government addressed the power crisis by securing temporary power production while at the same time rehabilitating its engines.

Chapter 2:

THE ELEMENTS OF OPPORTUNITY

So here we are at a point of transition here in the CNMI. While things may look dismal to some, there are pockets and pools of opportunity just waiting to be developed. Tips for spotting opportunity include recognizing trends, looking to the laws, following the "leaders", listening to the talk, watching the prices and consulting your own intuitive, passion-centered crystal ball. In this chapter are some random Saipan-specific, Tinian-targeted and Rota-rooted business ideas to get you thinking and asking the right questions. Each of these represents opportunity, when viewed the right way. But Saipan is also part of a larger world community. Within that larger community are factors that can, will and should affect the business opportunities on Saipan. Let's take a look at some global trends to help us figure out where to look for opportunity. But first, let me offer a few thoughts on what exactly we wish to accomplish by doing business on Saipan. Let me suggest a "prime directive."

The 10 Commandments of Paradise

Ever since arriving on Saipan and falling in love with its natural beauty, I've been working on some concepts to help everyone, not just those in power, maintain what we may often take for granted. I call them The 10 Commandments of Paradise. They represent a "prime directive" for business operation.

Viewers of the popular original Star Trek television series may be familiar with the term "prime directive" as the underlying guideline the starship Enterprise and all federation explorers had to abide by. According to Federation's prime directive, explorers were not allowed to interfere with the course of history on the planet they visited. For instance, they could not introduce technology, for instance, that was not indigenous to the planet they visited, because doing so would change the natural development of the life on that planet. Similarly, my 10 Commandments of Paradise are a basic underlying guideline for anyone seeking to do business on Saipan, with the goal of preserving something very sacred and invaluable.

In essence, the commandments suggest that the development and economic resuscitation that we pursue while doing business on Saipan must not perpetuate the cycle of decay. We must not lose our unique value in a misguided notion of what constitutes progress. We must never become so blinded by wealth that we miss the long-term effects of what we are doing to achieve it.

The 10 Commandments of Paradise

PREAMBLE: In the pursuit of progress, we must find solutions and make choices that ensure our survival, sustain our environment, honor our traditions, conserve our resources, respect our culture and preserve the right and ability of every generation to enjoy their lives in a natural environment in the same or better condition as that of the previous generation. Therefore:

1. We shall not allow industrialization to assume more importance than the individual, nor, in the pursuit of wealth and profit neglect what is in the best long–term interests of our own nation and its inhabitants.

2. We shall not let the unchecked depletion of natural resources nor the manipulation of the natural environment destroy our access to, nor our enjoyment of the pristine beauty of our land, sea and air.

3. We shall not allow another nation's political agenda to subvert our allegiance to truth and justice, nor influence us to make decisions not in our best interests.

4. We shall not allow another nation's interpretation of history to distort our own perspective, nor limit our right to advance our own.

5. We shall not allow another society's language, religion or education to overshadow our own.

6. We shall not allow misguided ideas of health and medicine to undermine time–honored traditions, nor our reliance on proven, natural methods of healing.

7. We shall not allow another society's concepts of entertainment, fashion, beauty, food or lifestyle to replace our respect for the fruits of our own.

8. We shall not allow another individual's or nation's concepts of morality to distort our own.

9. We shall not allow another individual's or nation's choices to influence our own sense of ethics.

10. And, in the pursuit of solutions to the challenges we will surely face in implementing all of the above, we shall endeavor to offer the world a new paradigm of progress, one that protects while it profits, one that elevates while not excluding, expands without exploiting, so that we can preserve paradise in the way we found it.

So, yes, you can call me an idealist. I'll wear the badge with pride. But I also believe that at the heart of idealism must be ideas. So I'd like to be part of those offering ideas for progress that don't perpetuate the negative aspects of capitalism. See, the trouble with capitalism is that it has traditionally been based on the depletion model, without regard to, or simply oblivious to the effects of the thrust for more and cheaper. As a result, our global society now experiences the effects of over-farming, overproduction, over-foresting, etc. on land, sea and air in the form of global warming, depleted soil, lowered air quality, rampant livestock disease and a host of ills.

Saipan, its leadership, and the new wave of Saipanpreneurs, in developing plans for the region, the economy, as well as the working and living conditions of its citizens, must develop ideas that preserve as well as profit; export without exhausting; selling without selling out.

And again, while I don't have the daunting task of leading a nation, creating economic models, or planning a society, I do know that in the implementation of any ideal, where there is a will, there is a way!

I believe that the old way is on its way out. I predict there will be a shift and a crumbling of industries and thought forms based on the depletion and exploitation models of progress. It's already happening in many areas. The people are ready for it. Indeed the world, as an entity, is starved for it. The old models will be replaced with models of sustainability, eco-friendliness, emission-reduction, etc. The CNMI can be one of the regions that shows the world the way.

So the questions we ask must change. Do we have anything other than cheap labor and tax incentives to offer investors? How can we preserve the balance and beauty of our islands even as we offer access to increasing numbers of tourists? How can we replace and improve even as we mine and export? How can we, as doctors do, practice our craft and reach our goals while doing no harm? How can we profit and leave things even better than how we found it? These questions have answers. The answers can be found by those brave enough to ask the questions and seek the optimal solutions outside of traditional ways of thinking….

Excerpt from The New Saipan Agenda
If you share my idealism, and would like to read more about doing business on Saipan from this perspective, download the full New Saipan manifesto[1] *at www.newsaipan.com*

Where to Look for Opportunity on Saipan

Someone asked me recently what sort of business I would start here on Saipan. To answer, I'd first like to introduce you to a term with which you're probably already familiar. The term is "catalyst." As you may remember from high school chemistry class, a catalyst is a substance that ignites, sets in motion, or speeds up a reaction without being affected itself. In life, every experience is a potential catalyst. Your flat tire, the argument with your spouse, and even your unhappiness at your job-all are potential catalysts. Because of the free will inherent in our experience here on the planet (we have the freedom to choose our responses), the reaction that a catalyst can spark is entirely under your control!

The purpose of catalysts

All catalysts are designed to offer a challenge or lesson.

There are only two possible paths one can choose from in response to a catalyst: It can be accepted or it can be controlled. The path you choose will be determined by your orientation. If you are oriented toward service to self (your own comfort), you will make one set of choices. If you are oriented toward service to others, you will see and choose from a different set of choices.

When faced with a catalyst it is important to understand that we are here to evolve in the direction of our orientation, and without life's catalysts, the desire to evolve and the faith in the process do not normally manifest and thus evolution does not occur. So don't rail against the changes and situations. Accept them as a natural part of the experience designed to help you grow.

Life is really that simple. Things happen. You choose your response based on your orientation. You evolve in the direction of your choice.

When neither path is chosen, the catalyst fails in its design and you proceed through life until some other catalyst appears which causes you to choose again toward acceptance and love or toward separation and control.

How to predict the future

It's a basic law of this dynamic, ever-changing universe that there's no such thing as something "staying the same." Things are either expanding or contracting, increasing or decreasing, getting better or getting worse. Even the metal or hard plastic computer or sheet of paper on which you are reading these words, as solid and as stable as they seem, are all slowly decaying and deteriorating. Come back in a few dozen years, and you'll see the effects of decay over time. If you know this, then you can look at everything from business phenomena to romantic relationships a little bit differently, and can perform what some might consider fortune-telling simply by asking, "Where is this heading?"

Every business, every situation, every relationship is either getting better or getting worse, growing or shrinking, going up or heading downhill. Therefore, as long as you can honestly assess what you observe or experience over a given time frame, you can "predict" where something is heading and take any evasive or remedial actions as necessary.

Now having said that, let's examine some current, observable facts and trends that will affect the future, and for which we have a choice of response.

1. The earth is going through changes.

Global warming is a reality. Temperature fluctuations are affecting access to water, arable[1] land and other resources for a growing segment of the world's population. These and other physical and climatic changes are observable.

2. "Peak Oil" is a reality.

The term "peak oil" refers to the peak in the world's oil production. The amount of oil available on the planet is finite. There is a point in oil production whether within a single oil field or the entire planet, when a maximum is reached. Once that maximum rate of production is reached, the rate of oil production (as well as the profitability of extracting it) on Earth will enter a terminal decline. The challenge this presents is that while the SUPPLY is declining, the DEMAND for oil (and the plastics, electricity, etc, which are oil-dependent) continues to increase as population and industrialization continue to grow. It's said that U.S. oil production peaked in 1970. World oil production, it is said by some, peaked in 2005. After a peak, production slows, profits decrease, and prices rise. You can already see the effects of this as gas prices start creeping upwards.

3. Corporate downsizing persists

More and more companies are outsourcing, downsizing and "off-shoring" in an effort to cut costs. Companies, particularly public corporations, are bound by their charters and by law to seek first the profitability of their shareholders. That's why the decisions these companies make often seem less humanitarian and more profit-inspired. That's because they have to be.

4. Global power and focus is shifting

China and India are growing economic forces. They represent sources of labor, consumers, as well as increased oil and energy demand. Companies the world over, in Europe and the United States, are importing laborers from China, or outsourcing skilled jobs to India.

Don't sleep!

As a potential entrepreneur, indeed as a nation, the opportunity exists to predict, anticipate, prepare for and position oneself for the effects of these trends. Don't wait for mainstream news broadcasts to confirm this. Don't expect politicians to make it part of their agenda in time. They are operating from a different agenda. Those who seek to rule the world are by nature unlike those of the world they seek to rule.

The challenge

As I said, there is always either a lesson or a challenge.

Within the context of these trends, the CNMI's economic condition, and by extension, your unique situation is a catalyst that provides an opportunity for you to respond in search of a lesson or a challenge.

As potential entrepreneurs, if we choose to rise to the challenge, using what we know about predicting the future, the question becomes first: What's going to happen as these trends and catalysts continue? And then more importantly, what shall I do in response to these happenings? Where should I look for the opportunity? What sort of business would I start? And finally which business path offers the most opportunity for service to others?

Now there are those who would ask, 'which path offers the most profit?', but that's a service-to-self orientation. We need a new paradigm. I suggest, as motivational speaker Zig Ziglar is credited with saying, that if you help enough people get what they want, you automatically get what you want.

My thoughts on a coming shift

There's another important trend that I believe is important to factor into this equation, and it is this: The continued growth upon which the current economic model is based cannot be sustained indefinitely. Infinite growth based on finite resources is unsustainable. Growth based on the exploitation of others is unethical and untenable.

Yes, China and India are both ideal sources of labor as well as the next great frontier for consumerism. The rest of the world's industrialized, market-driven, capitalist, consumer-oriented companies and entrepreneurs know this as well, and are rushing to position themselves.

However, the gold watch-sporting, cola-drinking, junk food-eating, luxury car-driving, soap opera-watching, video game-playing lifestyle upon which these companies rely to support their spiritually vapid, environmentally-depleting and mindless products, while exploiting the poor as the labor source, is on an inevitable decline. Global consciousness of a more serious nature is actually on the rise (it's just not being reported).

So if as a result, you see, as I do, the potential crash of the entire economic system upon which this model hinges, then you might agree that basing a new industry or business idea on such shifting sand, while perpetuating a soon-to-be outdated business model that separates and destroys the family structure, enslaves communities, while perpetuating indentured servitude is not a desirable course.

So, here is the challenge in a nutshell. The current model is unsustainable. We need to survive. However, our survival is based on buying into a definition of success that perpetuates the very model which is threatening our survival. What then, should be our best course of action?

The ethical paradox of selling survival

How do you survive in an economic system that is threatening your survival as well as its own? Answer: You sell survival. That's right, the game is changing to one of selling survival.

Right now others in the know are mobilizing to prepare to offer you their solutions. But what they offer won't be real solutions. They will offer products, services and a paradigm that perpetuates their control and their individual survival. In some parts of the world, companies are already charging the population for access to clean water, and some are selling seeds which have been genetically altered to produce single-generation crops, forcing farmers into a cycle of having to purchase new seeds every season just to survive.

But how do you survive in good conscience by profiting from what others need to survive? Therein lies the paradox of selling survival.

But that sort of response is not the option. Selling altered seeds or clean water is not the survival I wish to sell. If I were starting a business, I would follow the experts who predict that the stated trends will favor business models that:

1. Anticipate global shifts in social interaction and lifestyles (i.e. tribal living in larger social families that are self-supporting; ones that engage in more efficient means of creating energy, obtaining food, and supporting the common welfare)

2. Offer people the means of survival given the "peak oil" phenomenon (i.e. alternative fuel sources, power generation, solar, wind, insulating technologies)

3. Utilize technology in ways that empower and free the exploited from the manual labor that keeps them at the lower rungs of the totem pole.

These are just the tip of the iceberg, but there's enough there to start your own brainstorm on possible business ideas.

Wouldn't it be nice to jump ahead of the curve and start or join an industry, or launch a new business idea that helps the most people, prepares for coming earth changes, empowers rather than exploits the labor pool, reduces dependence on diminishing energy resources, offers the consumer real alternatives, while at the same time offers the world a new paradigm and consciousness as it relates to survivability, sustainability, adding our voice and actions to the very change in consciousness and alternate paradigm that our very survival necessitates? Yep, that would be pretty cool. And that's what I would do.

Following the Laws and Trends

Opportunities follow laws

If you want to position yourself for coming opportunities, find out what new laws and regulations are coming. Saipan recently passed a law requiring that future drivers log a certain amount of actual hours at a certified driving school. The result? An opportunity for a driving school that didn't exist before.

LAW: The recent announcement of a Department of Public Safety (DPS[1]) driver education requirement.

The new driver education requirement means that there is an opportunity for enterprising entrepreneurs to start their own Driver Training Schools. Do you speak Mandarin? Korean? Japanese? Those nationals need training too!

IDEA: Driver Education Training School; Contact DPS for the rules, regulations and requirements for setting up a Driver Training School.

Note: Public laws may be found archived at Northern Marianas Commonwealth Legislature website at http://www.cnmileg.gov.mp/

LEADER: Aquaculture

Another good tip for spotting opportunity is to look at already thriving businesses and provide ancillary products or services. It was serial entrepreneur Tony Pellegrino who offered me this one. Tony is the founder of Saipan Aquaculture, hatching, growing and exporting shrimp.

IDEA: Aquaculture support products and services

TREND: The garment factories are closing.

What does this mean for the foreign nationals on island? What does this mean for the actual buildings which housed the factories? Perhaps you can find some new uses for old factories. Warehouses, entertainment facilities, flea markets, and other ideas may work well.

IDEA: New uses for old factories

TREND: Gasoline prices are rising.

What change in consumer habits might this effect? Will people be driving less? Can you offer a way to get better gas mileage from existing vehicles? (do a search on "acetone") Will people be driving scooters and bicycles more? Is there a sustainable market for a bus-service on island?

IDEA: Sell fuel-efficient vehicles; Vehicle retrofitting; gas tank additives.

TREND: The Americans are coming!
What opportunities can this offer? Perhaps you can offer cultural sensitivity classes or programs for new arrivals about to live and work in the CNMI. Perhaps there are culturally-based products and services that new residents are looking for that you might offer. Are you the newest "Translator/Proofreader/Sign Maker/International Marketing Expert" on island?
IDEA: Offer goods and services for Americans

TREND: The Russians are coming!
If you listen to the talk around the island, you'll hear more Korean and Russian being spoken as tourists, business owners and new residents arrive.
IDEA: Offer goods and services

TREND: Need for funding both non-profit and profit-based businesses.
Whether it's government grants for renewable energy products, business subsidies for indigenous peoples, philanthropic donations for conservation efforts, there are sources of funding for which a good grant writer is always needed. You can offer your services as a "Proposal Consultant" specializing in government contracts or grants.
IDEA: Grant Writing

TREND: The Greening of America and the world
As industrialized nations awaken to the effects of global warming, there is increasing interest in promoting, producing and purchasing environmentally friendly, sustainably-produced products. A line of "produced in paradise" products which offer the world the opportunity to support local businesses while decreasing its carbon footprint might be a good idea. (A carbon footprint is a "measure of the impact human activities have on the environment in terms of the amount of green house gases produced, measured in units of carbon dioxide".)
IDEA: Export locally made, sustainable goods. Ideas include handmade soap, jewelry, bags, wood/paper/recyclable crafts, decorations, clothing and even food! Check out www.saipanpreneur.com for ideas and a place to sell your crafts.

TREND: Companies are downsizing.

Even though we are "part" of the U.S., we here on Saipan still represent lower-cost, offshore labor and skills that can be farmed out to overseas businesses. Whether it's a fully staffed call center or an individual who, with laptop and software, offer virtual assistant services to small and medium-sized businesses, the opportunity is there, thanks to the internet, to generate your income from clients overseas.

IDEA: Virtual Assistant; Business Support Services

TREND: Prices are rising.

If people don't have enough money to buy it, might they be willing to rent it? If they can't rent it, can they repair it? Cars and scooters aren't the only products this can apply to. The high cost of living might just open up opportunities to rent and repair a host of items.

IDEA: Rent & Repair

TREND: Ordering from Abroad

This one is a wild and crazy idea born from my own experience. If you've ordered products online from here on Saipan, you may discover that many companies don't, won't, or don't know how to reliably ship here to Saipan, Tinian and Rota, and other "exotic" locations. (i.e. The size of their operations means they can't guarantee the item will be sent Priority Mail, and/or they don't have the manpower to reliably attach the customs forms).

I've been thinking that a needed service would be to have a U.S. mainland location to provide re-shipping services to people here on these islands, and other unique destinations that big companies don't always ship to. That way, I could order something from a company, have it shipped to your location in the states, and then you send to me. Many people are already doing this using family and friends as their re-boxes, but there might be an increasing number of people whose friends and family just aren't reliable either. What do you think?

IDEA: Re-Box Services

The Business Idea Charts

Because the economic future of the islands is always a topic of conversation, there are always many ideas that float around during conversation. Everyone from tourists to children have their opinions about what's needed and wanted here on Saipan. Here, then, is a compilation of various business ideas as well as my opinion on their viability. Whether or not any of these ideas are viable for you in particular or here on Saipan, Tinian and Rota needs to be individually investigated and determined. However, they might offer a starting point for the savvy, opportunity-seeking entrepreneur to begin asking the right questions.

Key

Small—*The market is small given the lifestyle or the size of the target audience, or given that there are already enough businesses offering this product/service/*
Many—*Many exist. However, a business in this category could work with the right promotion or Unique Selling Proposition.*
Tour—*The local population may not be able to support this type of business, but it may be able to appeal to tourists.*
Open—*While there may be businesses in this category, the arrival of more expats could create a wide open opportunity for a savvy entrepreneur*

As we've noted previously, the major markets for doing business on Saipan are 1. Tourists, 2. a growing expat community, 3. a dwindling non-resident worker community, 4. local/indigenous base, and (often overlooked) 5. a global community via internet/worldwide shipping/export. Some basic products and services cut across all these markets and can be sold to everyone. Other products are unique to specific markets and care must be taken to market them appropriately.

1: Basic Products

Idea	Currently	Reason	Y/N
Air conditioners	several	New models, parts, service, repair. People may be cutting down on usage to save on power bills, but there's a captive market for someone who can offer great deals and great service	Maybe
Convenience Stores	Many dozens	Convenience stores located in underserved areas may do well. Stores which offer hard-to-find products and better customer service may also fare well.	Yes
Fast food restaurants	McD Subway KFC	Brand name recognition is a major factor in the success of a fast food. Wendy's didn't do well. McDonalds, however, continues to serve the island at two locations. I'd advise against it, but remember, I'm a vegan.	No
Hardware Store	4	GuangDong, Joeten/Ace serves the island well. The economy has slowed new construction.	Maybe
Hotel	30	Opinions vary, but the general consensus is that until the tourist industry improves, it's probably not a good idea to invest in another hotel.	No
Movie theatre	1	Saipan probably could not sustain another theatre. The current theatre already closed once recently.	No
Shoe store	2	There's a PayLess Shoestore on island that serves the island well, since most people wear "flip flops"….even the lawyers!	No
Video store	5 locally-owned outlets	Blockbuster recently went out of business here on Saipan. To make it affordable, movie rentals were priced (at a loss) at $2.99. The corporate office had to subsidize the loss, and eventually chose not to continue.	No

2: Basic Services

Business/Concept	Currently	Tried before?	Y/N
Airline	3	There exists a need for a low cost airline to service the Saipan-to-Guam travelers. The challenge is to offer service cost-effectively	Maybe
Auto Repair	Many, many	Like lawyers, auto mechanics are a staple of modern life. New car sales are down, but there's always a need to make the old look and run new.	Maybe
Bar & Grill	A few staples	Saipan nightlife consists of going to the local bar and mingling. A new idea, a great dj, activities, unique motif may just set you apart enough	Yes
Architect	Less than 5 listed	Much of the "design" of buildings is done by local craftsmen. There is definitely a need to upgrade the look of the island. Whether the market exists to support architects at this time is a little doubtful.	Maybe
Interior Design	one	See above	No
Insurance Co		Like lawyers and car repair shops, insurance companies are plentiful on Saipan.	Maybe
Internet Cafe	several	The college kids already have their hangout spot, the factory workers who used the cafes for video conferencing with those back home are gone, that leaves the grade school gamers with their lunch money to support the business. I say no.	No
Lawyer/Legal Services	Many, many, many	Immigration issues, labor issues, divorces, probate[1], it seems the world never has enough lawyers.	Yes
Mailbox rental	Five-ten	There is no home mail delivery, so everyone who expects mail needs a mailbox. There is a waiting list at the post office. Combined with other services, this could work	Maybe
Veterinarian	one	Contact PAWS[1] for more details to fully understand the vet situation on Saipan. http://www.paws-saipan.org/	Maybe

3. Things We'd Like to See:

Business/Concept	Comments/Opinion	Verdict
Aquaculture	This industry as been identified as a potential economy booster for Saipan	
Language Schools	"Where east truly meets west!"	Yes
Coconut Industry	You'd be amazed at what coconuts can spawn: vinegar, charcoal, oil.	
Produce Export	Tropical fruits, exotic herbs, spices, dried fruit, fish, shrimp to Guam, Asia and beyond! It's all possible. Experts believe Tarot would be a good export.	Yes
Green Energy	Hydropower, wave power, wind power, solar power	Yes
Retirement homes/services	Couples and singles in their 50s and 60s are attracted to Saipan for its laid back lifestyle and pace.	
Mushroom farm*	Possible export	Yes
Garment manufacturing	Yes, some have speculated that a reduced version of a garment industry could support the needs of the military on Guam—boots, uniforms, pillows, etc.	Maybe

4. More Things We'd Like to See:

Idea	Reason	Y/N
Language School	Saipan is truly where east meets west, and is uniquely geographically located for students from Asia and the Pacific region.	Yes
Internet-based design services	freelance design, book design, all sorts of design services which don't require face-to-face	Yes
Translation Services	With the mix of ethnicities and cultures on Saipan, there could develop outsourced translation services for a global market.	Yes
Mail order businesses	Generally, any business which gets its customers from off island has a better chance than those who rely solely on local clients.	Yes
Exporting Exotic flowers	Another possible export for Saipan.	Yes
New uses for old Garment factories	I've always thought "The Garment Factory", or "The SweatShop" would be great names for dance clubs/entertainment centers built in the old garment factories on Saipan	Yes
Permanent location for Sabulu Market vendors	Local farmers who sell their produce on Saturdays and Tuesdays need a permanent location.	Yes
Healing Center	This one requires a major shift in health consciousness, but there is a real need for real alternative healing on the island.	Yes
Herbal Medicines	See above	Yes

5. Still even more things we'd like to see

Idea	Reason
Bed & Breakfasts	I believe there is an opportunity offering alternative accommodations to tourists and visitors who don't wish to pay hotel prices.
Computer classes for local population	Subsidized, perhaps by government grants, this is a needed skill for a great segment of the population
Ethnic pastries	Local entrepreneur, Tony Pellegrino, thinks this is a good idea!
Chamorro, Carolinian Language School	With a small worldwide Chamorro population, and less than 5,000 Carolinians on the planet, there might be a cultural tourism connection for a language school based on Saipan.
Trade School	As the guest worker program phases out, there will be a need for skilled local workers to replace the loss in labor.
Saipan-specific arts/crafts/beadwork/ala Palau Storyboard	
Web-based products and services	If you can generate your income from a wider geographical area, you will put yourself in an increasingly recession-proof position
Cultural preservation programs	While the cultural and historical connection exists among the local population, there is a need for documentation and official recording.
Cultural Sensitivity Programs	Teachers arrive on island and are charged with teaching Micronesian youth without being aware of all the cultural nuances.
Storage Facility	I think this is a good idea as new people from the mainland come to the island.

6. Tourism Ideas

It's been said that tourism is the world's largest industry. Despite challenging times industry-wide, I believe that it is possible to carve out a niche and prosper here on Saipan. Those of us who live here are always recognizing opportunities for enhancing the destination to improve the overall tourist experience while boosting the economy. Everyone from taxi drivers to politicians to elementary school students have suggested a range of different activities, better marketing, new markets, and a different brand identity for the CNMI.

Long-time resident, Ruth Tighe, opines the following in her "On My Mind" column: *"What if Saipan were designated to fill a different but complementary niche in the over-all economy/tourism design? Saipan could - and does - provide the bulk of shopping opportunity. It provides most of the historic sites. It has large nature preserves. It has more golf courses, more sports offerings. It is the most metropolitan - in terms of potential cultural activities, business development and other urban pastimes.*

"The CNMI could be sold as an integrated whole - where one can go to the 'outer islands' primarily to gamble, with, on Rota, the added attraction of its garden beauty, on Tinian, its historic North Field, and then go to Saipan either to partake of its commercial offerings or to go trekking in its larger expanses of undeveloped "boonies." That would require better transportation among the three islands, but that is not an insuperable goal, and would surely provide more benefit, in the long run, for all three islands."

People have suggested increasing the number of child-friendly activities, making Saipan a conference-friendly destination, targeting the backpacker set, and more. I believe this opportunity is wide open with just a little creative thinking. Here, therefore, to help with the creativity, is a general list of types of tourism. I'm not endorsing any of these ideas in particular, but offer them merely to jump start the creative idea-generation process.

Tourism Ideas Checklist

A
Accessible tourism
Agritourism
Archaeological tourism
Atomic tourism

B
Benefit tourism
Bicycle touring
Birth tourism
Boat sharing
Bookstore tourism
Booze cruise

C
Campus tour
Christian tourism
CouchSurfing
Cultural tourism

D
Dark tourism
Day-tripper
Dental tourism
Disaster tourism
Dynamic packaging

E
Escorted tour
Excursion
Experimental travel
Extreme tourism

G
Garden tourism
Geotourism
Ghetto tourism
Grand Tour
Guest ranch

H
Halal tourism
Heritage tourism
Humane travel

I
Inclusive tour
Independent travel

L
LGBT tourism
Literary tourism

M
Medical tourism
Militarism heritage tourism
Music tourism

N
Nautical tourism

P
Package holiday
Pop-culture tourism
Poverty tourism

R
Religious tourism
Responsible Tourism
River cruise
Romance tours
Rural tourism

S
Sacred travel
Safari
Scenic route
Self-guided tour
Setjetting
Sex tourism
Shark tourism
Space tourism
Sports tourism
Spring break
Staycation
Suicide tourism
Sustainable tourism

T
Tolkien tourism
Tombstone tourist
Tourism geography
Travel to teach

V
Village tourism
Virtual tour
Volunteer travel

W
Walking tour
War tourism
Water tourism
Whale watching
Wildlife tourism
Wine tourism

7. Business and Industry Ideas

The following is a list of industries taken from a random Chamber of Commerce member list. Here are some opinions as to the viability of such a business.

Accommodations/Lodging	Many	Employment Services	Open
Accounting/Bookkeeping	Many	Engineering	
Advertising/Promotions*	Open	Entertainment	Open
Antiques	Tour	Environmental Products	Open
Apartments	Small	Financial Services	Open
Appliances/Service	Many	Florist	Small
Architect	Open	Food Processing	
Art/Galleries	Small	Food Services	Open
Attorneys/Legal Services	Many	Funeral Homes	Open
Attractions/Recreation	Open	Furniture	
Auto/Truck Sales	Small	Glass/Windows	
Auto/Truck/Motorcycle/Services	Small	Heating and Air Conditioning	
Bands and Music	Open	Home Improvement	Open
Banking Services	Small	Insurance	Small
Boutiques and Specialty Shops	Tour	Janitorial/Cleaning	
Builder/Developer	Open	Landscaping Services	
Business Services	Open	Mailing Services	Open
Candy/Ice Cream Shop	Small	Manufacturing	Open
Carpet/Rug/Floor Covering/Care	Small	Marketing	
Child Care	Open	Mortgage Services	
Chiropractic Services		Moving and Storage	Open
Cleaners/Laundries	Open	Newspaper/Magazine	Small
Coffee House/Juice Bar	Small	Office Supplies/Equipment	Open
Computer / Internet Services	Open	Optical/Optometrists	
Construction/Contractors	Open	Organizational Services	
Convenience/Liquor Store	Small	Organizations	
Counseling	Open	Outdoor Power Equipment	
Credit Services	Open	Painting Services	
Dance Studio	Small	Party/Home	
Delivery Service Messenger	Small	Pet Services	Open
Dental Services/Dental Labs	Open	Petroleum	Open
Distributor	Small	Photography	
Drug Store/Pharmacy		Physicians and Surgeons	Open
Educational/Tutoring	Open	Plumbing	
Electricians	Open	Pool and Spa Services	Open

Small = Market too small
Tour = Could work catering to tourists
Many=Many on island, but a standout could thrive
Open=open to new paradigm, export

Power and Utilities	
Printing/Publishing	
Public Services	
Ranching/Riding	
Real Estate	
Rehabilitation	
Rental Equipment	
Restaurants and Catering	
Retail	
Roofing	Open
RV Sales/Service	
Screenprinting/Engraving	
Security	Open
Seed Producers	Open
Signs	
Taxi Service	Small
Telephone Equipment/Services	
Television/Radio/Broadcasting	Small
Title Companies	
Travel Services	
Trucking	
Veterinarians	
Water Services	
Web Design	Open
Wholesale	
Winery	

Small = Market too small
Tour = Might work catering to tourists
Many=Many on island, but a standout could thrive
Open=open to new paradigm; export

NOTE: Now, don't be too influenced by my assessment of whether the opportunity for a particular business is "small," "open" or plagued by "too many" competitors. The truth is practically ANY idea is open, if you approach it the right way. Once you take some time to study the market from your unique perspective, you will undoubtedly see something that others don't see. You will be able to apply your unique passion to a solution in ways that others cannot. That is what will make the landscape and opportunity "open" and profitable for you. Take these assessments merely as an indication, perhaps, of where a little more creativity may be required in order to stand out.

Let the Grants show the way

Here's another unique way to brainstorm for business ideas. We already mentioned the need for grant writers. As you may know, the US government provides grants to encourage entrepreneurs to pursue certain specific types of research and business ventures. There are grants in the categories of community development, energy, environment, food and nutrition, cultural affairs, regional development and more.

☐ Visit the www.Grants.gov website for a wealth of ideas for which grants exist

Sell to the Military/Government

Here's another unique way to brainstorm for business ideas. We've already learned that the military is coming to Guam.

☐ Visit www.FedMarket.com for information on selling to the federal government

☐ Register as a contractor to sell to the federal government at www.ccr.gov

Brainstorm using the NAICS list

The North American Industry Classification System (NAICS) is the standard used by Federal statistical agencies in classifying business establishments for the purpose of collecting, analyzing, and publishing statistical data related to the U.S. business economy.

☐ Visit the "Business & Industry" section of the US Census Bureau website at www.census.gov, or go directly the list at http://www.census.gov/cgi-bin/sssd/naics/naicsrch?chart=2007

My opinion

Throughout history, many fortunes have been made in non-glamorous businesses like waste management, trucking and real estate. Here on Saipan, as we approach a new era, I believe that businesses focused on rebuilding the infrastructure from a green perspective will do well. Energy-efficient roofing, alternative power generation, and sustainable development in general should and could make a difference (and a dollar) here.

Ideas from the CNMI Government

The CNMI Government offers tax rebates and abatements to stimulate economic growth and development. Public Law 12-32, *the Investment Incentive Act of 2000*, authorizes the granting of rebates and/or abatements of up to one hundred percent (100%) for a period of up to twenty-five (25) years to qualified investors. The following are among the activities targeted by the Program:

- Franchise restaurants
- Water parks
- Aquariums
- Cultural centers
- Theme parks
- Resort hotels and condominiums
- Golf courses
- Convention centers
- Dinner theaters
- Special events
- CNMI based airlines and other related activities
- Manufacturing of high technology products
- Internet related businesses and/or businesses engaged in e-commerce
- Projects beneficial to the economic development of the Commonwealth

Ideas from the Chamber of Commerce

A recent economic report, made possible by a grant by the United States Department of Interior, suggests that Saipan is poised to successfully develop the following types of industries

- Financial Services Industry including trans-Pacific or intra-Asian trade, dollar denominated trust accounts, and securities exchange services.
- Free Trade Zone
- Captive insurance industry
- Data processing industry
- Software production industry
- Resource-based companies
- Small-scale commercial fisheries
- Pharmaceuticals
- Specialized higher or advanced education
- Retirement villages
- Forward deployment of US firms' Asian operations
- Store, transfer, and transshipment companies
- Telemarketing

Ideas from Ruth

Ruth Tighe is a model citizen. She's lived on Saipan since 1980. She was recently honored by the 16th House of Representatives which adopted a resolution for "her outstanding contributions to the CNMI as a professional librarian, writer, educator, and citizen..." and in "...building the literary wealth of the CNMI, raising the civic consciousness of the community, and offering present and future generations a model of excellence in public service and active citizenship."
She is best known for her weekly column, "On My Mind," an opinion piece that has appeared locally in one form or another since the mid-1980s, and can be found online at http://net.saipan.com/personal/omm, where you can also read more about Ruth and her contributions to CNMI society. (She is also featured on www.welovesaipan.com)

There is no shortage of great "what we'd like to see" business ideas within the community. Ruth's are some of the most inspiring. Therefore, the following are excerpts culled from her many columns over the years.

What to do with the Pacific Gardenia Hotel

Recently, the Commonwealth Development Authority (CDA) said it might take over Pacific Gardenia Hotel Sunset Bar and Grill (PGH) and operate the facility itself. What if, instead of contracting foreign workers - as would inevitably be necessary to run the place - the CDA wanted to REALLY help the local community and decided to repair and operate the place as a training institute for job-seeking local islanders?

It would take some coordination, but the CDA could hire skilled supervisors to teach local workers how to clean up mold, tear out carpets, prime and repaint rooms, etc. Chamber members or other businesses might be willing to donate the necessary equipment and supplies, or at least offer them at a reduced rate. Even if the workers were paid above local minimum wage, it would be cheaper than hiring dozens of foreign workers to do the same thing - given the added expenses that hiring foreign workers involves.

Similarly, once the hotel and restaurant have been restored, the CDA could hire experienced managers to train local workers in all aspects of running the hotel and its dining facilities, with the students, as they gained experience, being allowed to take over actual management duties in addition to the many other positions involved in operating a hotel, preparing and serving meals, maintaining equipment, etc.

It would provide jobs to many who are now jobless, or may soon become so. It would provide on-the-job, real-time experience to the students, giving them skills and training they could then use on the open market, as well as in their own homes.

PGH rooms and meals would be offered at reduced rates to anyone willing to put up with perhaps minor inconveniences in exchange for the lower room rate - baseball teams here to practice, the paparazzi here to follow Murai, visiting student groups, even tourists.

Since Northern Marianas College has just announced that it is dropping a number of certificate programs that would have been applicable to work-training at the PGH, it appears it would no longer be possible to hand out NMC certificates as reward for the students' efforts. But perhaps some other form of credit could be devised, either through NMC or the GED program, and perhaps NMC faculty could still be used for some aspects of the training.

What to do with the empty garment factories?

There's long been a need for a performing arts center on Saipan, and a friend suggested that perhaps one of the closed garment factories might lend itself to that purpose.

Of course, most of the factories are not in very desirable locations, but transforming one into a performing arts center might be a great way to rehabilitate a neighborhood. Even if in Lower Base - an area long abused, mis-used and under-used - placing an arts center there could work wonders for the entire area, and begin a process of revitalization as restaurants, souvenir shops, and related businesses opened around it.

The open floors of the factory would lend themselves to all sorts of stagings much more easily than the limited facilities now available on island, and still leave plenty of room for the storage of stage sets, costumes, equipment, etc. Nearby barracks could provide housing to off-island performers coming in to put on shows. With the building already in place, and presumably, utilities also in place, the costs of constructing a performing arts center would be greatly reduced, as would the time to get one operational.

There are apparently lease problems with making use of closed factories, but it becomes clearer every day that the longer those facilities are left empty and unused, the greater the loss to the lessor, be s/he government or private. Aggressive action should be taken to resolve the issues so that such assets/resources - of which the CNMI is in dire need - can be made use of, can be used to generate revenue. It might behoove the legislature to consider whether it can play a role in facilitating the re-use of all those empty premises. In fact, there's already one long-time resident who's said he would gladly manage the establishment and management of a performing arts center at no cost, should the CNMI establish one during his lifetime.

Saipan's Brand Identity

Others talk about finding a niche, a brand, that can identify and differentiate Saipan and the CNMI from other tourist destinations. Here, rather than a lesson from Guam, as DelaCruz suggest, the CNMI might better look at its neighbor to the southwest.

"Palau," says a headline in yesterday's *Marianas Variety* "will remain environment friendly." There isn't any reason the CNMI couldn't share that claim with Palau. The Micronesian Challenge began in Palau, but the CNMI supports it as well. The CNMI has already established marine protected areas. And they are working - the marine habitat is healing, the marine life increasing. With the increasing concern about global warming, sinking islands and declining species, wouldn't a tourist destination that advertised itself as actively addressing ecological concerns, as supporting the environment, as being ecologically accountable and responsive, be increasingly appealing? Why couldn't that be the CNMI's niche? All it would take is marketing of that angle, that perspective - along with greater support of it as well.

In fact, the CNMI could advertise opportunities for tourists to take part in the process. If tourists are on island during Beautify CNMI! cleanups, they could be invited along, to pick up trash, to paint over graffiti, to plant trees. Tourists could even be enlisted to help survey marine populations as they dive and snorkel - so they could feel part of the battle against global warming - and the campaign to restore CNMI waters to their former pristine condition.

Targeting the Affluent

Back on the home front, so to speak, one of the solutions to the problem of how to increase CNMI tourism revenues that keeps cropping up is to target wealthier tourists - the point being that per person, they would spend more dollars here than do the younger, less well-to-do tourists. The challenge is how to do that. How does one upgrade a destination that's long existed as accessible to anyone and everyone?

My guess is that accommodations would need to be more luxurious - large, well-appointed rooms with complementary fruit baskets and fresh flowers, great views out the windows, excellent room service, and deluxe special services, such as health spas complete with sauna, hot tub, masseurs, personal trainers, and, of course, outstanding food and entertainment. What little I've experienced of such accommodations, they're usually set off on separate floors dedicated to the well-to-do. It might even necessitate partitioning off parts of hotel beach front for special guests.

Numerous activities for such people are already available on island - from scuba diving and trail walking to golfing, sight-seeing and museum visiting. Though here too effort would have to be made to cater to a more exclusive category of tourist.

Naturally, all that costs a lot of money. And involves extra staffing. And then it would take intensive targeted advertising - not at the usual trade shows, but in exclusive magazines, like *Conde Nast*, or *New Yorker* or the *International Herald Tribune* or whatever else the moneyed classes read.

Given the high costs, and the dearth of investment dollars at the moment, is this something the Hotel Association of the Northern Mariana Islands could work on as a cooperative project of some sort? Or that the Marianas Visitors Authority could make a last-minute pitch for at the DoI conference in Hawaii?

It's a great idea. And it could work. If money could be found....

[For more, pick up a copy of Dan Kennedy's book *No B.S. Marketing to the Affluent*—Walt]

What Makes the CNMI unique?

The CNMI could become the "jewel' of the Pacific, a unique destination not because of its shopping or other commercial attractions, but because of its beauty and its cleanliness, its Commonwealth-wide ecotourism, its art, culture, history, its multi-ethnicity. Nature trails, pristine waters, organic farm products, environmentally-friendly hotels, transportation systems and facilities, indigenous handicrafts, cultural festivals, its "up close and personal" zoo, and responsible development of Chamorro, Carolinian, Spanish and Japanese historic sites, could all be marketed as unique to the CNMI, and form the basis of a new brand, a better image, to be marketed to prospective tourists. As just one example, Saipan has several sites relating to the period of the Japanese Mandate - yet to date, these have all been ignored in favor of developing only the war-related sites. Might not more Japanese tourists be interested in that aspect of the history of their country in the CNMI than in its war history?

MVA (Marianas Visitor's Authority) may be relying on exit surveys to formulate its plans, but if tourists don't know what else of interest may or could be available on island, how can they ask for it? MVA might better focus on working with on-island agencies, the community, to increase and improve island attractions - and on developing rainy day activities. Take the Northern Islands, for example. Not mentioned at all, anywhere. Yet they offer great potential for true eco-tourism. Moreover, something is wrong when tourists say they want greater restaurant experiences, even though Saipan already has a wonderful variety of good restaurants - most of whom, in fact, suffer from a lack of patronage....

What to do with the La Fiesta Mall?

Asked for comments, this past week, on the idea of using part of the governor's "white elephant" (that is, the La Fiesta Mall) as a junior/senior high school, and thinking again of how inappropriate that setting was for use as classrooms - be they community college or public school - it suddenly occurred to me what that space would be good for. The idea came while thinking about how La Fiesta was designed, trying to understand what the original planners must have been thinking about.

If one recalls how it looked in its prime - with fountains, and twisting canals, and quirky, whimsical art here and there, like the dolphins jumping up out of the concrete, and the extensive landscaping with blooming flowers and color everywhere, the conclusion is inescapable. The traffic wasn't supposed to be orderly, logical, but rather, random. The intent was to make it a visually-pleasing, visually interesting, place to visit.

Like an art gallery. Or a museum. La Fiesta Mall would be an ideal place to put that catch-all building - museum plus historic preservation office plus arts council - currently (and inappropriately, in my opinion) planned for the flood-prone Garapan wetlands area. Its former shops could easily be converted into art gallery showrooms, or museum exhibit space, with relatively little re-modeling.

There'd be ample room for work space and for storage (in La Fiesta I, for example) for all the museum's and the HPO's (Historical Preservation Office) artifacts. And ample room for exhibits - it wouldn't be necessary to take down one exhibit in order to mount another - for either the museum or the arts council. Instead, there would be lots of room for permanent exhibits, for exhibits of individual artists, themes, eras.

La Fiesta could also accommodate the performing arts. There already is a large outdoor amphitheater setting. One of the larger places, such as the former Tony Roma's, could be converted into another performance area. The entire mall, in other words, could become a combination arts/historical institute - a center for the performing and visual arts as well as historical museum. There might even be room for natural history displays.... And there'd be room for all the administrative offices as well.

Admittedly, art galleries, museums, usually do organize their exhibits in some kind of pattern, but the order doesn't have to be rigid. Exploration, wandering, random sorties into one exhibit room or another are all typical - and often encouraged - modes of behavior in such settings. For this, La Fiesta is ideal. And the random whimsical art already there, the visual attractiveness of the place - as originally designed - fits right in with that kind of use.

With so much space - if all three buildings were used - there'd also be room for some nice cafes or restaurants, where people could come in and rest their feet and have a snack - to think about what they'd seen, or collect the energy to see some more - at any time of day, not only between 7 a.m. and 10 a.m., or 11 a.m. and 2 p.m., or after 6 p.m., hours that many restaurants keep. And there'd be room for museum shops, for individual artists' show rooms, for selling handicrafts and art supplies and other related items. In fact, wouldn't it be wonderful to also have one of those multi-museum shops that sell replicas from a number of major art and history museums - not only from the U.S., but from museums throughout the world!

Such an offering would appeal to those Japanese tourists who, according to a recent Marianas Visitors Bureau poll, were disappointed with shopping choices on Saipan, saying they could find much of the same merchandise back in Japan. But items from the Smithsonian museums, from the various fine arts museums in major U.S. cities, from art and history museums in countries around the world, are not found in Japan, and would be a real drawing card for shoppers not only from Japan, but for tourists everywhere in Asia. The same would be true of handicrafts, not just from Micronesia, but from Asian countries, or South America, or Australia and South Pacific islands. The availability of such items could add a whole new dimension to the attractiveness of the CNMI as a tourist destination.

To establish and maintain a quality image appropriate to such an undertaking - rather than one of kitsch and cheap tourist junk such as the crushed coral and resin souvenirs currently found not only in the Duty Free Shops but all over island - would require oversight from a knowledgeable board with the good taste to judge wisely, and with full, absolute, authority to screen and monitor candidates for space in the mall so that galleries, exhibits, restaurants, shops, and offices all were true to the concept of a highly reputable world-class arts institute.

No poker parlors would be allowed. No porn shops or massage parlors. No 99 cents, or $3 stores. McDonald's might be ok, but only if no yellow arch dominated the scene.

A big project. But one with huge potential. The CNMI could use the CIP funds that were going to build the museum/arts complex in Garapan to re-model La Fiesta, probably at considerable savings. Those savings could then be applied to building a school that was designed for use as a school, rather than trying to adapt a site so totally unsuited for school use. Can you imagine, for example, the many windowless classrooms students would be forced to use at La Fiesta? Nor does La Fiesta have room for athletics - for a baseball field or a track, or basketball courts.

Yes, tourists would have to be bussed to La Fiesta. But they are already bussed everywhere else. Perhaps this is the point at which consideration might finally be given to allowing locals on those busses as well - at least if they wanted to go to the art/history museum complex.............

And yes, it's a radical idea. But at least it would preserve what had been the mall's original intent. It would make use of, take full advantage of, all the money, and all the labor, that has gone into its landscaping. (And if its generating plant - which allegedly is the most efficient on island - were also preserved, as it should be, that would take full advantage of the expertise and expense that went into its design as well.) It would bring a desirable form of development to the northern end of the island. It would preserve and maintain the complex, rather than degrading and destroying it.

For more of Ruth's Saipan commentary visit *http://net.saipan.com/personal/omm*

....and the best idea of all: turn your passion into profit!

Any one of the ideas in the previous charts could lead to business success here on Saipan. So, how do you decide what's the best option for you? Ultimately, you will always be more successful and more personally fulfilled when you start a business for which you have a personal passion.

My book, *Turn Your Passion Into Profit* (ISBN: 0974531324), offers a step-by-step guide for discovering your passion, aligning it with your purpose, creating a viable product or service, and marketing it for profit. It's based on the philosophy that:

> *"If you create and market a product or service through a business that is in alignment with your personality, capitalizes on your history, incorporates your experiences, harnesses your talents, optimizes your strengths, complements your weaknesses, honors your life's purpose, and moves you towards the conquest of your own fears, there is ABSOLUTELY NO WAY that anyone in this or any other universe can offer the same value that you do!"*

And, when you create unique value in the market place, you can be practically assured that people will beat a path to your door or your store to buy what you're selling!

Once you determine the particular area and expertise that interests you, then expand the possible business ideas by applying your particular purpose to it. On my website (www.passionprofit.com) is a personality test which helps you determine if your purpose in life is as a "creator," "savior," "guru," or "guide." What this will help you determine, for example, is how best to maximize any given business idea. Say, you determine you have an interest in local crafts. If you are a "creator," you may be happiest simply making the thing. If you are a "savior," you might offer some sort of healing therapy in the form of arts and crafts. If you are a "guru," then your business might be as a crafts instructor, teaching people the fine art of craft making and selling. If you are a "guide," you may find yourself collecting and offering museum displays as a way of preserving, promoting and advancing the culture.

Chapter 3:

SAIPAN SECRETS

The Psychology of Doing Business on Saipan

So, now you have an idea of what sorts of businesses might work here on Saipan. But wait! Before you leap headfirst into your venture, you need to know something about the lifestyles, habits, tendencies, business traditions, protocol, history, mindset and worldview of the people who call Saipan home. These are the challenges you'll face in launching and sustaining your business here.

Top 10 Lifestyle and Buying Habit Secrets you need to know to Do Business on Saipan

1. Just because Saipan is a small island, and just because people will drive past your establishment 10 times per day, doesn't mean that they know where you are and what you do. Even though word of mouth is powerful, you cannot rely solely on it to get the word out about your business.

2. There are many different and unique publics on Saipan. The Filippino market is different from the American market, the Korean market and the Thai and Chinese markets. Unless you have a very commonly used, basic product, you may find that you are frequented by the American market exclusively. Each market has different world views, different needs and different disposable incomes. Each group moves in entirely different circles. Food sells to everyone, but wind turbines will only sell to Americans.

3. Unless you strike a deal with a tour company to bring tourists (especially Japanese) to your establishment, you may have a challenging time reaching the tourists. They are typically shuttled around in tour buses, and rarely simply strike out on their own. The exception are the Russians, who come independent of tour guides and are more likely to venture around town on their own.

4. Even though Saipan is very small, people who've lived here for a few years begin to adopt an even smaller circle of travel. People in Kagman find it "too far" a trip to venture into Garapan (just 5 miles away). People may spend years in one little town and never venture to the other side of the island.

When I lived in Bronx, New York, I traveled the 5 miles down the Bronx River Parkway, the 4 miles across the Cross Bronx Expressway, and the 10 mile length of the island of Manhattan to get to my favorite vegetarian Chinese restaurant in lower Manhattan's Chinatown. When I lived in Manhattan, I traveled the 28 miles to get to IKEA to go furniture shopping. And when I lived in Silver Spring, MD, I traveled four hours and 300 miles to visit friends in Brooklyn, NY. Now that I live in As Matuis on the north end of Saipan, I find that driving the 6 miles to party in Garapan is just WAY TO FAR! I'm told it happens to many people who live here. One's sense of acceptable distance gets recalibrated to island distance. Something to be aware of when planning the location of your business on Saipan!

5. There is no foot traffic on Saipan. Everyone drives or is driven around. In the past and currently, many food stores, for example would provide transportation in the form of vans to shuttle customers (primarily contract workers living in barracks) to their stores to do their shopping.

6. Many locals and Americans and Filippinos purchase items by catalog and/or through the web. Amazon.com is a favorite shopping place for items which cannot be purchased on island.

7. Another strategy for disposable income shopping is a trip to neighboring Guam. People take day trips to Guam to shop for any and everything not available on Saipan.

8. There is no residential mail delivery on Saipan. "Everyone" has a post office box, and goes to pick up their mail at either one of the official US postal service stations, or at an agency/establishment that rents mailboxes.

9. To understand making money on Saipan, you need to look at the numbers on Saipan. As a relatively isolated island, the numbers of residents, contract workers and visitor/tourists are an essential part of the mix. When Saipan had the approximately 34 garment factories doing business here, there were approximately 15,000 garment workers (mostly from China) who lived here. This resulted in money going to CUC (Commonwealth Utilities Corporation) for electricity for the factories and barracks. Neighborhood stores benefited from customers purchasing food, clothing, appliances, etc. Banks benefited from the workers' savings on deposit. These institutions hired employees. Airlines benefited from occasional trips "back home." The government benefited from taxes and fees paid by the factories. Shipping companies benefited from the factories sending their products overseas. Incoming containers with products for residents could be filled on the outgoing leg of their back and forth journey. (At present, shipping companies have had to raise the prices of incoming container shipments, as there is no outgoing business to make up for the losses.)

With the departure of the garment industry, the tourist industry is invested with much hope to rescue Saipan. That's why the military build-up on Guam is looked at with so much hopefulness.

In essence, Saipan's success as a viable business center relies either on a sizable local resident population, or a vibrant visitor population. That's why it is important to create a strategy that reaches as many people as possible either inside or outside of Saipan.

10. Beware the law of the fad.

"I've seen it before," says Pam Halstead, Business License Officer at the Dept of Finance on Saipan. "Something new comes on the island, people rush to it for a while, and then the excitement fades away."

Top 10 Mindset and Worldview Insights you need to know to Do Business on Saipan

1. Despite the existence of the American flag, this is NOT America!

2. Respect the Chamorro and Carolinian cultures as the host cultures.

3. Remember, many contract workers (who actually comprise the majority of the population) are on Saipan to earn money to send back to their families in other countries. They typically won't spend money on the luxuries that Americans will.

4. Green consciousness, and the will to follow through with the requisite behavior exists within a very small segment of the population.

5. If you do come to Saipan with the goal of offering an alternative of some sort, prepare for a unique and personal observation. Sometimes in life, people will prefer the familiar "screw" to the unfamiliar alternative. Loyalties here (at least among certain segments of the population) appear to run along familial and party lines. This will, perhaps, be the most important awareness that may (but doesn't have to) discourage you. Stay away from people who've been here too long. People with the best of initial intentions, but without the strength of character to weather the inertia that grips the majority of the population, end up throwing up their hands, and just joining in step with the masses--accepting the familiar screw, and not feeling empowered enough to do anything about it. You must stay strong and persevere.

6. The small town feel and mindset (arguably a good thing, compared to the impersonal, anonymous life one finds in big cities), may at times be a hindrance to the market-driven assurance, and expectation that the "better" mousetrap will win out. Here, "the mousetrap my "daddy/benefactor/employer/investor" tells me to buy" may often be the one that wins.

7. There is no population group known as "everyone on Saipan." In other words, just because an establishment is open for business on Saipan, it doesn't mean it will ever be patronized by the full range of all the groups on the island.

Your population target is NOT the 60,000 to 80,000 people on island. Depending on who you are and what you are selling, it may never be the 10,000 Chinese, or the 20,000 Filipinos, or the two Jamaicans on the island.

8. Language and culture play an important part in the success of a business on Saipan. Unless you are Chinese, familiar with the market, the lifestyle, the language and the cultures of the Chinese residents, you may never have a Chinese person step through your door.

You won't find any Chinese in non-Chinese restaurants, unless they are with an American. You won't find many Americans in SunLeader (a Chinese market), unless they are with a Chinese person. You'll rarely find Chinese in the American clubs. You're not likely to see a Bangladeshi at a local strip club. You'll likely see Filippinos at a majority of the establishments for several reasons. As the predominant English-speaking contract workers, they will typically be the employees at these establishments. As a result, other Filippinos will be aware of the establishment. Also, as English-speakers, and the largest segment of the population, Filippinos tend to be in relationships with Americans and other English speakers, thus facilitating their integration into the "mainstream."

9. People with different information, make different decisions.

Despite the perfect storm that is raging on Saipan, there always seems to be new construction, new businesses being launched. Many of these bold entrepreneurs are simply building for a hoped-for future. Many others, however, have access to information that others do not. Your awareness of trends. Your inside track to the plans of others. The golf-course speculations and strategy of those in the know, create a different playing field.

10. Familiarity breeds sales

As in any small town, it's often the case that people will do business with you, refer their friends and family, once a relationship is established.

Federalization Secrets & Predictions

How will federalization affect the business climate on Saipan, Tinian and Rota? That is, of course, the big question on everyone's collective mind. The answer, of course, is unknown. As of fall 2009, much of the detail of the actual transition to federal immigration and labor has yet to be determined. We can, however, make a few educated guesses given certain scenarios.

First, let's get a clearer picture of what is being proposed in a broad sense. When Saipan's immigration is taken over by the United States federal government,

Contract workers who currently use their work permits as a means of entry to the CNMI will no longer be able to do so. The same entry requirements that govern the US mainland, Guam and other US territories will apply to Saipan.

Another aspect of federalization involves the gradual increase of the minimum wage for workers here on island. The minimum wage that employers must pay their employees is currently $4.55/hour with a scheduled increase of $0.50 every six months until the wage matches the federal standard in the mainland: $7.25/hour. That is expected to occur in 2015.

Along with federalization has come a new regulation. As you may be aware, Department of Homeland Security (DHS) and Department of Justice regulations have recently been updated to amend the definition of the geographical "United States" to now include the CNMI for immigration purposes. Prior to this update, people with US permanent resident alien status ("green cards") who came to the CNMI were considered technically "outside" of the United States, and, if they stayed too long, would risk being in violation of the terms of their green card status that requires they maintain continuous residence in the geographical United States for a specified number of months each year.

In other words, it hasn't been just the distance that has kept some US mainlanders away from Saipan. For those green card holders who wished to become US citizens, their time in the CNMI DID NOT count towards their residency requirement. Now it will.

What this means is that once word gets out that Saipan is now part of the US (and as the minimum wage approaches national levels), green card holders living in the US, or even on Guam, might consider coming to Saipan to live and work providing a new influx of residents and labor.

[See also "Tony's Take on Federalization" in Bonus Chapter 7]

10 Conversations about Life on Saipan That will Affect Your Business Success

Regardless of your circle of contacts or the industry in which you plan to do business, if you aspire to live and work on Saipan, you'll most likely find yourself having most or all of these conversations at some point in time. These are conversations based on observations about how things were, how things are, and how things ought to be on Saipan. Everyone from students to politicians who care about the future of Saipan find themselves sharing their opinions in these conversations.

The reality as well as the perceptions these conversations point to will have an effect on who your customers are, how you reach them, how quickly you launch and grow your business.

Even this section, written with the goal of preparing you for life on Saipan, will not adequately prepare you for the reality of the actual experience. You may wish to return to this section after spending a few months or years on Saipan to compare your new perception with what you are now thinking reading this for the first time.

1. Small Town, Marianas

Saipan is essentially a small town in the middle of the Pacific Ocean. If you've never lived in a very small town, and especially if you're coming from a major metropolis like Tokyo or New York, there are some things to know. People know each other. People talk. There is no anonymity. People have histories and reputations that precede your arrival on the island.

2. Transparent Saipan

Because of its size, the culture, the nature of the immigration and visitors to the island, there are things that people know about you before they ever meet you. As stereotypical as it sounds, people on Saipan have a 99% chance of guessing your occupation and intentions just by looking at you. If you're Bangladeshi, you're most likely a taxi driver or a security guard. If you're a Chinese lady, you're most likely a garment factory worker or massage parlor employee. If you're a Black male, you're most likely one of the military personnel stationed on the ship anchored off Saipan's coast. If you're a white female, you're probably a teacher. Local Japanese residents look and dress differently from Japanese tourists. Russians walk differently than white Americans. In a small town, everyone knows who the new persons are. They stick out like sore thumbs.

3. Father Federal

The CNMI receives billions of dollars in aid from the United States federal government. Some say that this historically paternalistic relationship with the United States' federal government has stifled the development of a vital entrepreneurial spirit within the island.

4. Mother Japan

As the source of the majority incoming tourists to Saipan, Japan is touted as a significant pillar of the CNMI economy.

5. Brother Guam

"Is Guam a better, more desirable tourist destination than Saipan? Sure, there's more to do there. It's bigger. It's part of the US. We even go there for the shopping! Why does the US often lump us together with Guam? We're a completely different nation. Our diving is better. We have a more natural, more authentic paradise island experience. Guam is too commercialized. We still have our indigenous spirit."

6. Rivalries, Loyalties and Suspicions

These are touchy subjects. Simply by mentioning them, we run the risk of perpetuating what should be non-issues. However, it may at least be of historical significance to know that there've been said to be rivalries between the Chamorros on Guam and the Chamorros on Saipan; the Filippinos and the Chinese; suspiciousness towards whites by the indigenous people; disdain for Korean business practices. Even if unfounded, and merely opinions and perceptions, these perceptions themselves are significant enough to be powerful influences on life on the island.

7. Corruption.

Corruption exists on Saipan. There. I've said it.

Now, having said that, I honestly do not believe there is any more corruption and deceit here on Saipan than on Wall Street or in Washington DC. In fact, having seen the police reports of crime on the island, I can say that it is actually less, per capita.

What I do believe is that the thefts look bigger given the relative size of the island. When I first landed on Saipan, I listened to the local news reports to get a feel for the island. I recall quite vividly one of the first news reports I heard on local Saipan television. It seemed a tourist's laptop had been stolen. Imagine! It made the news! When was the last time you heard a Tokyo, Hong Kong or New York television news story about one person's stolen laptop? That's just a testament to the relative rarity of crime, the small town feel of the island, as well as the importance placed on creating a pleasant tourist experience for visitors to the island.

I also believe that the corruption appears larger given the fact that for the outside world that reports on it, it seems out of proportion to the size and relative importance of the island. Keep in mind, very few people in the United States know about Saipan. I, myself, had never heard of it prior to 2005, and now here I am writing a book about it. As a result of its relative obscurity, it is still seeking an identity within the minds of the public as well as the media. This is important to understand, because when people first hear things about an unknown place, the thing they hear becomes part of that place's identity, and since news tends to be negative to boost ratings, the things you first associate with a foreign place tend also to be negative.

If I say, "Jonestown, Guyana," the average American has no other frame of reference other than the Jim Jones mass suicide reported in the news in the 80's. If the Bernard Madoff investment fraud scandal had been based on Saipan, it would have been a tremendous blow to the island's reputation because little else is known about Saipan. No one associates Madoff with his hometown of Queens or with the upper east side of Manhattan where he lived. Neither Queens nor Manhattan now suffer a bad reputation as a result. It's simply a crime without a hometown. Saipan, however, in its quest for an identifying trademark, brand identity, relevance and space in the public consciousness, is now associated with Jack Abramoff, garment factories and labor abuses and corruption. News stories about beautiful beaches, laid back lifestyle, world class diving and amazing sunsets weren't abundant or compelling enough to stick in the public's mind.

8. Foreign Labor and rising minimum wage

People contend that business on Saipan is doomed as the minimum wage rises. That will likely be true for many businesses whose profit margins can't support paying higher wages. However, the increased minimum wage will usher in a new era of business and prices and margins.

9. The high cost of shipping

When the garment industry departed, Saipan lost more than just user fees[1] from the factories' operations. As exports decreased, the cost of importing containers had to rise to meet the shipping companies' expenses. I mentioned this in the section entitled "Disadvantages of Doing Business on Saipan."

10. Family Ties

Anyone who lives here long enough will have conversations about the importance of family names on Saipan. A local person's lineage will say much about who he is, who she will vote for, and where her loyalties may lie.

Secrets for Reaching Customers on Saipan

Here on Saipan, there are only 5 ways to reach your English-speaking customers on Saipan. Here is my take from most to least effective.

1. Word of Mouth
2. Radio ads
3. Newspaper ads
4. Television
5. Text Ads
6. Blogs

1. Word of Mouth—Like anywhere else, this is the most effective form of marketing.

2. Radio Ads: It doesn't cost anything to turn on a radio. With only 5 stations catering to specific audiences, this might be the best bang for your buck.

3. Newspaper Ads: Probably less effective simply because the newspapers cost money, and its easier to listen than to read.

4. Television: Many people are out enjoying the Saipan weather rather than inside watching television. When they do, except for the local news hour on the local network, there are likely many cable options which would make television advertising less effective.

5. Text ads. This medium has not yet been fully explored. Because of the low cost, people on Saipan probably use text messaging more than any other form of communication . My prediction is that text message marketing will be a vital service for future business owners. You can learn more at www.saipantext.com.

6. Blogs. There's a new generation of residents who follow their friends' exploits on Facebook™ and personal blogs. I predict this will prove to be a good way to reach the more connected and younger markets on Saipan.

Tip: A good advertising campaign should seek to communicate in English, Korean, Tagalog (Philippines), Japanese, Chamorro and Carolinian.

*****

So, now you have your business idea. You have a little better idea how the people think and act. You have your marketing strategy. What's next? The easy part: setting up your business on Saipan.

Chapter 4:

STARTING A BUSINESS ON SAIPAN

- Who can Start a Business on Saipan?
- Zoning, Part 1
- Legal Business Structures
- The CNMI Business License
- Special Licenses
- Alcoholic Beverage & Tobacco Licenses
- Gaming and Amusement License
- Professional Licenses 1 & 2
- Sanitary Permit
- Banking License
- Insurance License
- Special Requirements for Bankers and Insurers

Who Can Start a Business on Saipan?

IMPORTANT
As of November 28, 2009, immigration into the Commonwealth of the Northern Mariana Islands will be administered by the United States federal government through the Department of Homeland Security. For the latest update on how this affects investor status on Saipan, visit www.dhs.gov.

Anyone except a current CNMI contract worker can start a business on Saipan. US citizens and permanent residents of the United States can start a business on Saipan. A national of any country can apply for investor status.

The charts which follow show the requirements and fees for the various certificates and entry permits which may be applied for by those seeking to do business on Saipan.

Item	Fee & Terms	Required
☐ **Short term entry permit** *ATB (Authorization to Board) letters and Short-Term Business Entry Permits are available to persons coming to the CNMI temporarily to engage in negotiations, formulate plans, survey prospects, submit bids, etc. They may not hire employees or be locally compensated for work.*	$0	• Short-Term Business Entry Permit Application is to be completed at the Immigration Areas at Saipan, Tinian, Rota airports upon entry.

Business and Investment Certificates

Item	Fee & Terms	Also Required
☐ **Regular-Term Business Certificate** *Regular Term Business Certificate holders are admitted for a period of up to ninety (90) days within a twelve (12) month period.*	$200 The Regular-Term Business Certificate Application must be submitted ten (10) days prior to the expiration of the permit or a penalty of one-hundred dollars ($100) per day is assessed for each day the application is late.	• Police Clearance from country origin • Copy of Passport • Copy of Current Health Certificate • Original Landing Form 958 • Copy of Return Airline Ticket • Copy of filed, current Annual Report • Articles of Incorporation • Copy of Business Proposal or Plan • Copy of current Business License • Birth Certificate • Marriage Certificate, if applicable • Two (2) current 1.5" x 1.5" photos.
☐ **Long-Term Business Certificate** *The Long-Term Business Certificate allows foreign investors to lawfully engage in business in the Commonwealth for two (2) years.*	$1,000 The Long-Term Business Certificate Application must be submitted ten (10) days prior to the expiration of the Business Entry Permit or 958 Landing Document, Short Term Business Entry Certificate or a penalty of one-hundred dollars ($100) per day is assessed for each day the application is late. • Evidence of paid $150,000 capital by foreign investor (bank statements showing amount deposited in CNMI accounts, invoices, receipts or contracts for assets purchased, stock purchase transaction records, loan or other borrowing agreements, money transfers, promissory notes, security agreement, or any other agreements supporting the application)	• Original Landing Form 958 or permit • Copy of filed Artic of Incorp, By-laws and Certif of Incorporation • Copy of filed Annual Report (Exist) • Copy of the initial Annual Report/new • Copy of Business License(s) • Business Financial Statement • Personal Financial Statement • Lease Agreement • Sketch of Business Location • Inventory of Assets • Bus Gross RevTax Return last 3Q • Filed copy Form 1120 Corp Tax Rep • Employee Withholding Tax (if applic) • Notarized labor compliance form (• Consent to Release of Account Info • Security Bond Deposit of $25,000 • Three, 1.25" x 1.25" current photos • Marriage Certificate, if applicable • Current Police Clearance from country of origin. Clearance for Korean nationals will be requested by the Dept of Commerce • Current Health Certificate • Copy of Passport • Copy of Birth Certificate

Item	Fee & Terms	Also Required
☐ **Foreign Investment Certificate** *The Foreign Investment Certificate grants foreign investors the right to lawfully engage in business in the CNMI as long as the investors are in compliance with the standards of issuance.*	Certificate Fee: $10,000 Investor Visa Fee: $2,500 Evidence of paid $100,000 per person in an aggregate investment in excess of $2,000,000 or $250,000 by an individual in a single investment. (bank statements showing amount deposited in CNMI business accounts, invoices, receipts or contracts for assets purchased, stock purchase transaction records, loan or other borrowing agreements, money transfers, promissory notes, security agreement, or any other agreements supporting the application) As required for the Regular and Long-Term Business Certificates, the Application for an Approved Investment must be submitted ten (10) days prior to the expiration of the applicant's current business certificate or Landing Form 958. For each day the application is late, a penalty of one-hundred dollars ($100) will be assessed.	*• Original Landing Form 958 or orig permit* *• Copy of filed Articles of Incorporation* *• By-laws, Certificate of Incorporation* *• a copy of filed Annual Report (if existing)* *• a copy of initial Annual Report (if new)* *• Copy of Business License(s)* *• Business Financial Statement* *• Personal Financial Statement* *• Lease Agreement* *• Sketch of Business Location* *•Inventory of Assets* *• Bus Gross Rev Tax Return last 3 quarter* *• If applicable, Employee Withholding Tax* *• Notarized labor compliance form (if appl)* *• Consent to Release of Account Info* *• Certificate Fee of $10,000* *• Investor Visa Fee of $2,500* *• Three (3), 1.25" x 1.25" current photos* *• Marriage Certificate, if applicable* *• Current Police Clearance from country of origin. The Department of Commerce will request clearance for Korean nationals.* *• Current Health Certificate* *• Copy of Passport* *• Copy of Birth Certificate* *All submitted in triplicate*

Entry and Investment Applications and Instructions Mentioned in this Section That You May Need

Tip: Print this list, ☑ check all that apply and carry with you

- ☐ Short-Term Business Entry Permit Application
- ☐ Regular-Term Business Certificate Application
- ☐ Long-Term Business Certificate Application
- ☐ Long-Term Business Certificate Application Checklist
- ☐ Consent to Release of Account Information
- ☐ Standard Operating Procedures (for Long-Term Business Certificates)
- ☐ Application for an Approved Investment
- ☐ Foreign Investment Certificate Checklist
- ☐ Reference Handout in Preparing Application for Foreign Investment Certif
- ☐ Standard Operating Procedures (for Foreign Investment Certificates)

For the most current copies of all forms and reference materials, contact The Department of Commerce's Foreign Investment Office at:

Foreign Investment Office
CNMI Department of Commerce
Caller Box 10007
Capitol Hill, Saipan, MP 96950
Tel.: (670) 664-3017/8-Saipan; 532-9478-Rota; 433-0853-Tinian
Fax: (670) 664-3067-Saipan; 532-9510-Rota; 433-0678-Tinian

Zoning, Part I

• The first stop in the process of starting a business on Saipan is to get Zoning Board approval for your intended business. A new zoning law was passed which targets certain areas on the island for certain types of businesses, and limits the type of businesses you can operate in other areas. You will not be able to do business on Saipan unless your type of businesses is "zoned" (i.e. allowed) in the area you choose. Download the complete 2009 Zoning Law and maps at zoning.gov.mp

We'll get into more detail about the zoning approval process in the chapter on setting up your physical location.

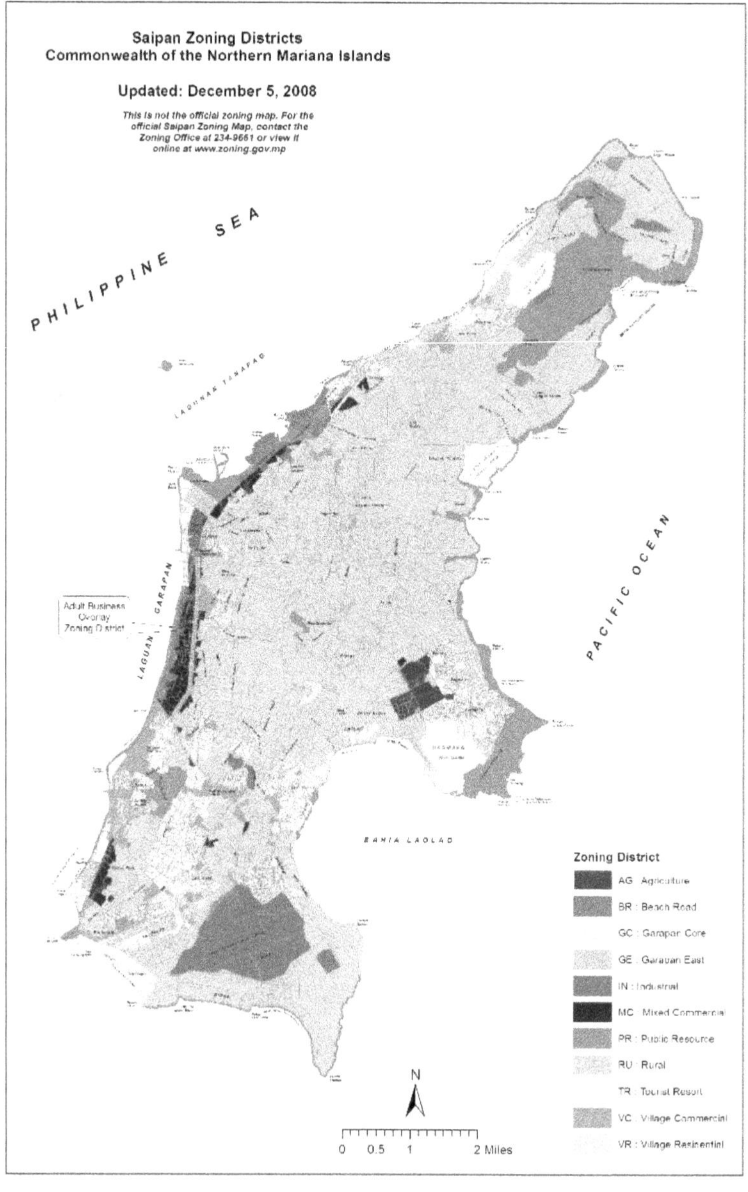

Legal Business Structures

Anyone doing business on Saipan has a choice of legal structures to choose from when forming a business in the CNMI:

- Sole proprietorship
- Partnership (General or Limited)
- Corporation (C or S)
- Limited Liability Company (Partnership or Corporation)

Each structure has its own legal and tax differences. In deciding which structure to establish, investors should consider these differences along with the type of business activity, individual circumstances, business goals, and other personal and financial factors. It is highly recommended that practicing attorneys and accountants be consulted before deciding which type of business structure is appropriate for the individual investor and the company. A list of attorneys and accountants may be found in the local Yellow Pages. This section highlights the format and registration requirements for the legal forms of business in the CNMI.

☐ SOLE PROPRIETORSHIPS

As the name implies, sole proprietorships have one business owner. They are the easiest and least expensive to establish since legal formalities are not necessary. Fairly simple in structure, sole proprietorships are subject to minimal government regulation and reporting requirements.

Proprietors or owners have complete control over the business, receive all profits or incur all losses of the business. Sole proprietorships and their owners are treated as single entities. Owners, therefore, are personally liable for all business debts; liability is not limited to the value of the business.

Sole proprietors need not register with the Registrar of Corporations before applying for a CNMI Business License.

☐ PARTNERSHIPS

The two types of legal partnerships in the CNMI are: general and limited. A general partnership has two or more owners sharing management and liability of the business but is not incorporated. Partners control the operations of the business and have unlimited liability for business obligations. The business actions of any one partner binds other partners. Hence, partners are liable for each other's actions.

A business with one or more general partners with the same rights and responsibilities and one or more limited partners playing passive roles in the business is a limited partnership. Limited partners do not actively participate in the management of the business to avoid being personally liable for the debts of the business. The most a limited partner may lose is the amount of his/her investment in the partnership.

Generally, partnerships require more time and money to create than sole proprietorships as it may require the drafting of partnership agreements.

Registration Procedures for Partnerships

Partnerships must register by submitting to the Registrar of Corporations a Partnership Registration Form. The Registrar of Corporations requires partnerships to file the Annual Partnership Statement. For more information about registration procedures and reporting requirements for general or limited partnerships, contact:

☐ CORPORATION

C-Corporations and S-Corporations are the legal forms of corporations in the CNMI. The primary reason for incorporating is to minimize personal liability. Corporations are legal entities separate from the individuals that own or operate them; they have their own assets, liabilities, rights and privileges. Considered the most complex and time consuming to create, investors should consult with a practicing attorney in establishing a corporation.

Corporations have incorporators, shareholders, directors, and officers. Shareholders have limited liability in both C- and S-Corporations. Should the business fail, be sued, or go bankrupt, the liability stops at the corporate level. Corporations can perform many business functions without directly involving the shareholders or owners of the corporation.

The difference between C- and S-Corporations relates to tax issues. Although the CNMI tax system mirrors the Internal Revenue Service Code, substantial differences exist relative to local tax rebates and other matters. Investors are strongly urged to seek the advice of the Division of Revenue and Taxation, a certified public accountant, or other tax authority in determining the impact of taxes on the different business structures.

Registration Procedures for Foreign Corporations

Foreign corporations register by completing and submitting an Application for Certificate of Authority to the Registrar of Corporations. The application and an official certificate that verifies that the corporation exists in good standing with the country or state of its formation must be submitted to the Registrar in triplicate. This certificate must be obtained from the appropriate office in which the original company was registered and presented with an English translation where applicable. The Registrar will not accept application packages without proof of payment to the CNMI Treasury of the filing fee of one-hundred dollars ($100). Once this fee is paid and the incorporation documents meet statutory requirements, the Registrar will file and return a file-stamped copy of the documents and a Certificate of Authority to the corporation.

Registration Procedures for Domestic Corporations

Domestic corporations are required to submit Articles of Incorporation and By-laws of the Corporation in triplicate to the Registrar of Corporations. As specified in the Checklist (for Registration of Domestic Corporations), the Articles of Incorporation must set forth:

- the name of the corporation containing the words: "Corporation," "Incorporated," "Company," or "Limited" or their abbreviations
- the number of shares that the corporation is authorized to issue
- the address of the corporation's initial reg'd office and name of initial agent
- the name and address of each incorporator

The Articles of Incorporation may also set forth:

- the names and addresses of individuals who will serve as initial directors
- provisions inconsistent with the law regarding the purpose or purposes for which the corporation is organized; managing the business and regulating the affairs of the corporation; defining, limiting, and regulating the powers of the corporation, its board of directors, and shareholders; a par value for authorized shares or classes of shares; the imposition of personal liability on shareholders for the debts of the corporation to a specific extent and upon specific conditions

Once the filing fee of one-hundred dollars ($100) is paid and the incorporation documents are in order, the Registrar of Corporations will file the documents and prepare for issuance the Certificate of Incorporation.

Registered Office and Registered Agent

All corporations must continuously maintain a CNMI registered office and a registered agent. The registered office may be the same as any of its places of business. The registered agent may be a resident of the CNMI, a domestic corporation or a foreign corporation authorized to transact business in the CNMI.

Registered agents must sign the

☐ Consent and Authorization to Appointment as Registered Agent.

This document gives consent to service of process only and does not include liabilities and obligations of the corporation. The consent and authorization is valid for one (1) year. If a corporation is without a registered office or agent in the CNMI for sixty (60) days or more, the Registrar of Corporations may commence a proceeding to administratively dissolve the corporation.

Reporting Requirements

Corporations registered in the CNMI must file a

☐ Annual Corporation Reports

with the Registrar of Corporations. The initial report must be filed within sixty (60) days after the domestic corporation was incorporated or the foreign corporation was authorized to transact business. Subsequent reports must be submitted between January 1 and March 1 of the following calendar years. A filing fee of fifty dollars ($50) must be made with the CNMI Treasury before annual reports are submitted to the Registrar in duplicate.

Change or Dissolution

To register any change in a corporation, an authorized person must complete

☐ Application for Amended Certificate of Authority

for foreign corporations or an Application for Amended Certificate of Incorporation for domestic corporations and submit it to the Registrar of Corporations along with proof of payment to the CNMI Treasury of the filing fee of fifty dollars. Applications for Amended Certificate of Authority must be accompanied by an official certificate verifying that the corporation exists in good standing in the country or state of its formation. Applications for Amended Certificate of Incorporation must be submitted with applicable articles of amendment, articles of restatement, or amendment of by-laws.

Investors who want to reinstate a revoked or administratively dissolved corporation must file, in duplicate, an

☐ Application for Reinstatement of Revoked Corporation, or an

☐ Application for Reinstatement of a Corporation Administratively Dissolved

along with a

☐ Certificate of Compliance from the Department of Finance's Division of Revenue and Taxation

certifying that all taxes owed by the corporation have been paid. The filing fee for reinstating a revoked or an administratively dissolved corporation is one hundred dollars ($100).

To register cancellation or dissolution of a corporation, an authorized person must complete an

☐ Application for Certificate of Withdrawal

and submit it to the Registrar along with proof of payment to the CNMI Treasury of the filing fee of twenty-five dollars ($25).

☐ LIMITED LIABILITY COMPANY

CNMI Public Law 14-11 added limited liability companies (LLCs) as another form of legal business structure in the CNMI. An LLC combines several features of corporation and partnership structures. It has a separate legal existence and generally offers liability protection to its owners or members.

LLCs can be classified as either a partnership or corporation for tax purposes. Investors are urged to seek the advice of the Division of Revenue and Taxation, a certified public accountant, or other tax authority on the tax advantages for this type of business structure.

Registration Procedures for LLCs

LLCs must register by filing with the Registrar of Corporations Articles of Organization and paying the required $100 filing fee.
Foreign LLCs register by submitting an

☐ Application for Certificate of Authority - Foreign Limited Liability Company.
The original application plus two (2) copies must be submitted with the required $100 filing fee and a

☐ Certificate of Existence or similar record duly authenticated by the Secretary of State or like official of the state or country under whose law it is incorporated.

Reporting Requirements

The Registrar of Corporations requires that initial annual reports for LLCs be filed within 60 (sixty) days of incorporation for domestic LLCs or issuance of the Certificate of Authority for foreign LLCs. Subsequent reports must be filed on or before March 1st of each year. The filing fee for annual reports is $50.

For filing requirements for partnerships, corporations, and LLCs, contact:

Registrar of Corporations /CNMI Department of Commerce
Caller Box 10007
2nd Floor, Joeten Commercial Building, Room 27
Dandan, Saipan, MP 96950
Tel.: (670) 664-3002; Fax: (670) 664-1015

For information on the Certificate of Compliance (necessary for the application to reinstate revoked or administratively dissolved corporations), contact:

Division of Revenue and Taxation/CNMI Department of Finance
P.O. Box 5234 CHRB
1st Floor, Joeten Commercial Building
Dandan, Saipan, MP 96950
Tel.: (670) 664-1000-Saipan; 532-1040-Rota; 433-1600-Tinian
Fax: (670) 664-1015-Saipan; 532-0473-Rota; 433-1615-Tinian

The CNMI Business License

<table>
<tr><th>Item</th><th>Fee</th><th>Required</th></tr>
<tr><td>☐ **Business License**

Businesses need a license to operate in the CNMI.

Business Licensing Office
Division of Revenue and Taxation
CNMI Department of Finance
P.O. Box 5234 CHRB
2nd Floor, Joeten Commercial Bld
Dandan, Saipan, MP 96950
Tel.: (670) 664-1000-Saipan; 532-1040/1065-Rota; 433-1600-Tinian
Fax: (670) 664-1015-Saipan; 532-0473-Rota; 433-1615-Tinian</td><td>

Business Type	Fee
Banks	$500
Banks (Offshore)	$1000
Insurance Agents	$75
Insurance Brokers	$100
Insurance Company	$300
Manufacturers	$50
Public Utilities	$300
Security Dealers	$300
Scuba Instructors	$100
Scuba Diving Tour	$100
Produce/Fish vendors	$5
Wholesalers	$50
General Business	$50

</td><td>• Application for Letter of Compliance and/or Tax Clearance from Division of Revenue & Tax
• Certificate of Clearance from Workers' Comp Commission*
• Sketch of business location
• Proof of payment of business license fee(s) to CNMI Treasury.

• Partnerships: copy of company's Partnership Registration Form.

• Corporations applying for first time: copies of the company's Certificate of Incorporation, Articles of Incorporation, and By-laws.

• Partnerships and corporations: submit a file-stamped copy of company's most recent ann report.

• Non-U.S. citizens must provide their Immigration Status.</td></tr>
</table>

The Workers' Compensation Certificate of Clearance certifies either: 1) that all workers are covered by workers compensation insurance or 2) that the business has no employees subject to such coverage. Business License Office personnel will review your application for completeness and advise you of when to pick up your license. At the time of issuance, you should receive a business license for each business activity and your tax identification number.

Any change in ownership, in the lines of business, or other information contained in the original Application for Business License must be reported to the Business License Office within ten (10) working days of such change. For more information on the Workers' Compensation Certificate of Clearance, contact:

Workers' Compensation Commission
NMI Retirement Fund
P.O. Box 501247
2nd Floor, NMI Retirement Fund Building
Capitol Hill, Saipan, MP 96950
Tel.: (670) 664-8024-Saipan; 532-9516-Rota; 433-3733-Tinian
Fax: (670) 664-8074-Saipan; 532-9486-Rota; 433-3863-Tinian

Alcoholic Beverage & Tobacco Licenses

Name of License	License Fee	Required with application
☐ **Alcoholic Bev Control License** *Businesses that manufacture or sell alcoholic beverages or tobacco products must first obtain an Alcoholic Beverage Control License or a Tobacco Control License to engage in such manufacture or sale.* *Other requirements relating to condition of premises, sale restrictions, registration of employees, renewals, and prohibitions of sale may be obtained from* Alcoholic Beverage and Tobacco Control Division CNMI Department of Commerce Caller Box 10007 Capitol Hill, Saipan, MP 96950 Tel.: (670) 664-3026/3065-Saipan; 532-9478-Rota; 433-0853-Tinian Fax: (670) 664-3061-Saipan; 532-9510-Rota; 433-0678-Tinian	Applications that are received between Oct and Dec in a given year are assessed the full amount of the applicable fee. Applications received between January an d March are assessed three-fourths of the applicable fee while those received between April and September are charged one-half of the applicable fee.	• Corporation: Certificate of Good Standing • Corporation: Corporate documents *(i.e. Certificate of Incorporation, By-laws, Articles of Incorporation, Annual Corporation Report)* • Corporation: Alcoholic Beverage Control License Application - Exhibit "A" • Current Police Clearance/Criminal Record for persons listed on Exhibit "A" of the Alcoholic Beverage Control License Application, bartenders, business partners and proprietors •Partnership: copy Partnership Agreement • If application is for a Class 3 type license, the Class 3 Retail Dealer's On-Sale General Registration Form, copies of work and entry permits for non-resident workers and the Social Security Numbers and official I.D. for resident workers • Non-US citizen: copy of Non-Immigrant Long-Term Business Entry Permit • Copy of Public Health Sanitation Permit • Copy of Business License • Business Location/Site Drawing • Copy of notarized Lease/Rental Agreement, Title or Deed referring to the proposed premise to conduct business • Receipt of $25 Filing Fee

<table>
<tr>
<td>☐ Tobacco Control License

Wholesalers, retailers and distributors of tobacco products must have a Tobacco Control License to engage in operations. There are six classes of the Tobacco Control License.</td>
<td>
<table>
<tr><th>Type</th><th>Class</th><th>Fee*</th></tr>
<tr><td>Wholesalers</td><td>1</td><td>$300</td></tr>
<tr><td>General</td><td>2</td><td>$100</td></tr>
<tr><td>Vending</td><td>3</td><td>$100</td></tr>
<tr><td>Distributor</td><td>4</td><td>$100</td></tr>
<tr><td>Temporary</td><td>5</td><td>$50</td></tr>
</table>
*+$5 application fee

Valid for one year
Renewable annually</td>
<td>• Current Police Clearance/Criminal Record
• List of names of employees or agents authorized to sell tobacco items. 18 yrs+
• Photocopy of ID of employees or agents
• If applicable: Pub Health Sanitation Permit
• Copy of Business License
• If propty owner, copy Lease/Rent Agrmnt
• Applicant's Busi Location/Site Drawing
• Payment receipt of the $5 Application Fee
• Payment receipt of applicable license fee</td>
</tr>
</table>

Businesses may need to obtain licenses from government agencies or organizations such as the Alcoholic Beverage and Tobacco Control Division, the Banking Office, the Insurance Commission, the Bureau of Environmental Health, the Department of Finance or the Casino Gaming Commission before engaging in their activities

Gaming and Amusement Licenses

Type	Fee	Application Requirements
☐ **Gaming/Amusement Machine License** *The CNMI Department of Finance also regulates the commercial operation of gaming and amusement machines.*	(see fee table below)	CNMI Department of Finance P.O. Box 5234 CHRB Capitol Hill, Saipan, MP 96950 Tel.: (670) 664-1100/01-Saipan; 532-1040-Rota; 433-1600-Tinian Fax: (670) 664-1115-Saipan; 532-0473-Rota; 433-1615-Tinian
☐ **Casino License** *Casino operations are legal in Tinian only. Casinos are licensed and regulated by the Tinian Casino Gaming Control Commission.*		Tinian Casino Gaming Control Commission P.O. Box 143 Tinian, MP 96952 Tel.: (670) 433-0063 Fax: (670) 433-9290 *contact@tiniangamingcommission.com* *www.tiniangamingcommission.com*
☐ **Lottery License** *The CNMI Department of Finance licenses and supervises lottery operations.*		

Gaming/Amusement Machine License fees:

Type	Fee
Coin-op Phono	$150
Coin-op CD	$150
Other music	$150
Kiddie ride	$25
Pachinko	$6000
Poker	$12000
Pool tables	$150
Video games	$150

Businesses may need to obtain licenses from government agencies or organizations such as the Alcoholic Beverage and Tobacco Control Division, the Banking Office, the Insurance Commission, the Bureau of Environmental Health, the Department of Finance or the Casino Gaming Commission before engaging in their activities

Professional Licenses Part 1

<table>
<tr><th>Name of License</th><th>License Fee</th><th>Required with application</th></tr>
<tr>
<td>☐ Various Professions

Architects, engineers, land surveyors, real estate appraisers, plumbers, electricians, carpenters, harbor pilots, barbers and beauticians obtain professional licenses or certification from the Board of Professional Licensing</td>
<td>Application requirements and associated fees vary by trade and type of license/certificate</td>
<td>For specific details, contact:
Board of Professional Licensing
P.O. Box 2078
House #1336
Capitol Hill, Saipan, MP 96950
Tel.: (670) 234-4811/4809
Fax: (670) 234-4813</td>
</tr>
<tr>
<td>☐ Nursing License

Nurses must receive licensure from the Commonwealth Board of Nurse Examiners before practicing nursing in the CNMI. Registered and practical nurses may be licensed by examination or endorsement. Contact:

CNMI Board of Nurse Examiners
P.O. Box 501458
Capitol Hill, Saipan, MP 96950
Tel.: (670) 664-4810/4812
Fax: 664-4813</td>
<td><table>
<tr><th>Type</th><th colspan="2">Application by Exam/Endorse</th></tr>
<tr><td>Registered</td><td>$80</td><td>$60</td></tr>
<tr><td></td><td></td><td></td></tr>
<tr><td>Practical</td><td>$60</td><td>$40</td></tr>
</table>
Fees should be made payable to “the CNMI Treasurer.”</td>
<td>• <u>Application for (Nursing) License</u>
Plus:
•Official transcripts high school/nursing sch
• Birth certif., marriage certif, if applicable
• Payment of non-refundable proc. fee.
•Two 2” x 2” photos taken within 6 mos. Applicant signature on bottom of photo
Depending on the type of license being applied for, the Board may require:
A verification of license
A copy of current license
Evidence of 30 hours of Continuing Education completion over past 2 years
Certified copy current CNMI employ contract Certified copy of previous nursing employment over past nine mos</td>
</tr>
</table>

☐ **Medical Profession Lic** *Acupuncturists, chiropractors, clinical psychologists, dental nurses hygienists, dentists, medical laboratory technologists, optometrists, pharmacists, physical therapists, radiologists and other healing arts practitioners must first obtain licensing from: Medical Profession Licensing Board* c/o Commonwealth Health Center P.O. Box 500409 C.K. Capitol Hill, Saipan, MP 96950 Tel. (670) 664-4811 Fax: (670) 664-4813	Requirements and fees vary by profession. Fees should be made payable to "the CNMI Treasurer."	Applicants should expect to submit: • Completed application; • One (1) 2" x 2" photo. Photo must be signed by applicant and current; • Applicable fee • Notarized copy school diploma • Notarized copy current license, name of issuing authority; • Name, tel, address previous employer

Businesses may need to obtain licenses from govt agencies or organizations such as the Alcoholic Beverage and Tobacco Control Division, the Banking Office, the Insurance Commission, the Bureau of Environmental Health, the Department of Finance or the Casino Gaming Commission before engaging in their activities

Professional Licenses Part 2

Name of License	License Fee	Required with application
☐ **CNMI Attorney License** *To be licensed to practice law in the CNMI, contact the CNMI Bar Association*		For specific details, contact: CNMI Bar Association P.O. Box 504539 Saipan, MP 96950 Tel.: (670) 235-4529 Fax: (670) 235-4528 Website: www.cnmibar.net
☐ **Taxicab Operator License** *Persons interested in engaging in a taxicab operation must be licensed by the Department of Commerce's Bureau of Taxicabs.* *Bureau of Taxicabs* *Division of Enforcement and Compliance* Dept of Commerce Caller Box 10007 C.K. Capitol Hill, Saipan, MP 96950 Tel. (670) 664-3014; Rota: 532-9478 Tinian: 433-0853	*Other requirements relating to insurance, vehicle registration, taximeter, rate schedule, and ID renewals apply.* Fees should be made payable to "the CNMI Treasurer."	• Application for Certification of Fitness and Taxicab Operator's ID Card. • Criminal Record Search • Traffic Record Search • Copy of Passport and/or Birth Certificate • Valid CNMI Driver's License • Three (3) 2" x 2" photos • Health Certificate • Sketch of Location • Copy of Bureau of Motor Vehicles Taxi • Operator's License • Receipt of Payment of Bureau of Taxicabs Identification Card - $15.00

Businesses may need to obtain licenses from government agencies or organizations such as the Alcoholic Beverage and Tobacco Control Division, the Banking Office, the Insurance Commission, the Bureau of Environmental Health, the Department of Finance or the Casino Gaming Commission before engaging in their activities.

Sanitary Permits

Businesses Required to Apply

Sanitary Permits

Sanitary permits are required of numerous types of businesses to enforce health and sanitation standards and to prevent the outbreak or transmission of diseases.

- ☐ Businesses that sell, serve, distribute, store or process food or drinks (i.e. cafeterias, restaurants, bars, taverns, retail stores, wholesalers, roadside vendors, ice plants, butcher shops, etc.)
- ☐ Businesses that provide room accommodations (i.e. hotels, motels, apartments, boarding houses, staff housing, room rentals, etc.)
- ☐ Shops or clinics where there is contact between employees and patrons (beauty shops, barber shops, massage parlors, pedicure, manicure shops, tattoo shops, dental clinics, eye clinics, acupuncture clinics, sanitariums, and other health clinics)
- ☐ Institutions (i.e. schools, day care centers, gyms, correctional facilities, etc.)
- ☐ Vehicles used for the commercial transport of foods or drinks (i.e. pizza delivery vehicles, road-side vending vehicles, wholesale delivery vehicles)
- ☐ Commercial vessels and ships
- ☐ Swimming pools
- ☐ Sellers of cosmetics and cosmetic devices

Permit Fee

Category	*Fee*
Eating/Drink	
Restaurant	*$50*
Snack bar	*$50*
Café/Coffee shop	*$50*
Canteen	*$50*
Food Processing	
Kitchenette	*$80*
Luncheonette	*$50*
Cafeteria	*$50*
Drinking Establ	
Bars	*$70*
Karaoke lounge	*$70*
Night Club	*$70*
Tavern	*$70*
Refreshmnt stand	*$50*
Retail Food Store	
Mom & Pop	*$50*
Convenience store	*$80*
Market	*$80*
Minimart	*$50*
Sale of cosmetics	*$50*
Sale of refreshmnt	*$50*
Manufactured food	*$50*
Processed food	*$50*
Roadside Vendor	
Produce	*$50*
Fish	*$50*
Fish & Produce	*$50*
Room/Accomm	
Hotels 1-50 rooms	*$80*
Hotels 51-100 rms	*$90*
Hotels 101+ rooms	*$130*
Motels	*$80*
Apartments	*$80*
Staff housing 1-10	*$80*
Staff housing11-20	*$90*
Staff housing 21+	*$130*
Boarding house	*$80*
Room rental	*$80*

Permit Fee

Category	*Fee*
Food Processing	
Meat & Food	*$80*
Water & Ice	*$80*
Other (bakery)	*$80*
Wholesale	
General Merch	*$80*
Storage facility	*$80*
Shops & Clinics	
Barber shop	*$50*
Beauty shop	*$50*
Barber & Beauty	*$50*
Massage Parlor	*$50*
Optical clinic	*$80*
Facial/Manicure	*$80*
Dental Clinic	*$80*
Sanitarium	*$80*
Health clinic	*$80*
Sauna/Jacuzzi	*$80*
Educational	
School	*$130*
Day care center	*$130*
Transportation	
Delivery Vehicle	*$50*
Snack mobile	*$50*
Other	
Duplicate permit	*$30*
Ship clearance	*$85*
Deratting certific	*$110*
Fly trap	*$30*
Food hand certif.	*$20*
Food hand temp	*$20*
Food hand duplica	*$10*
Condemned food	*50/hr*
Food hand training	*$250*
Cruise ship clear	*$350*

Penalties:

Follow-up inspection due to non-compliance: $50

Resume ceased ops: $330

Expired permit: $55/mo

NOTE: New businesses must visit the Bureau of Environmental Health (BEH) to schedule and request for an inspection of the business. In two weeks or less, BEH will conduct an inspection. At the inspection, BEH inspectors will request to see the following:

- CNMI Business License;
- Certificate of Occupancy issued by the Department of Public Works; and
- Food Handler Certificate(s), if required.

Food Handler Certificate Process

Food handlers at eating and drinking establishments must obtain the Food Handler Certificate before working at such establishments.

Application Requirements and Procedures

1. Food handlers may pick up the Food Handler's Certificate Application at any CNMI licensed clinic. At the clinic, applicants undergo health screening. Physicians performing examinations will provide BEH the Food Handler Screening Examination (Report).

2. After the examination, food handlers should contact the BEH to schedule attendance at the Food, Hygiene and Sanitation Workshop.

3. Upon completion of the workshop, the applicant/workshop attendee will receive a Certificate of Completion for Workshop Participation. The Food Handler's Certificate Application must be completed and submitted to a BEH representative at the workshop.

4. When submitting the application, the applicant must bring a photo identification (i.e. passport, driver's license, alien registration card or other form of picture identification). An employment contract may also be required to verify employment date with business/employer. Upon receiving normal or good health screening results, BEH will contact applicants and ask them to bring into the BEH Office their Certificate of Completion for Workshop Participation. The Food Handler Certificate will be issued once the certificate fee is paid.

5. Food handlers must give their certificates to their employers to be kept on file at the place of employment. During sanitation inspection, employers will be asked to show these certificates. The Food Handler Certificate is valid for one (1) year and must be renewed forty-five (45) days before expiration.

Duplicate Certificates

Food handlers with valid Food Handler Certificates may request for duplicates of the certificate for a fee. See Table 2.3. For more information on Sanitary Permits, health and sanitation standards, and Food Handler's Certificates, contact:

Bureau of Environmental Health
Division of Public Health
Department of Public Health
P.O. Box 500409 C.K.
Navy Hill, Saipan, MP 96950
Saipan: (670) 664-4870/4848/4898; Fax: (670) 664-4871
Rota: 532-9461; fax: 532-0955
Tinian: 433-0395; fax: 433-9247

Banking License Pre-application Procedure

*See also: Special Requirements for Bankers and Insurers

☐ 1. File Notice of Intent to Organize

Before any stock subscriptions are made, incorporators must file with the Director of Banking a notice of intention to organize a bank in the CNMI. The notice of intention must include:

• the name, residence and occupation of each incorporator and the amount of stock subscribed and paid for by each

• the name and address of an individual within the Commonwealth to whom notice to all the incorporators may be sent

• the total capital, the number of shares of each class and the par value of the shares of each class of the proposed Commonwealth bank

• statement on whether it is intended that the proposed Commonwealth bank shall have trust powers

• the municipality in which the proposed Commonwealth bank is to be located

Stock subscriptions may be made thirty (30) days after filing of such notice.

☐ 2. Apply for Charter

After the stock capital is fully subscribed, incorporators may apply for a charter. The proposed charter must include:

• the name of the proposed Commonwealth bank

• statement on whether it is intended that the proposed Commonwealth bank shall have trust powers the island on which the proposed Commonwealth bank it is to be located

• the amount of capital, the number of shares of each class, the relative preferences, powers and rights of each class, the par value of the shares of each class and the amount of the paid-in surplus

• a statement whether voting for directors shall or shall not be cumulative and the extent of the preemptive rights of stockholders

• other proper provisions to govern the business and affairs of the Commonwealth bank as desired by the incorporators.

NOTE: Three (3) copies of the proposed charter must accompany the Application for Charter of a Commonwealth Bank. Incorporators must mail notice of this application to each bank doing business on the island in which the proposed bank is to be located and to persons and organizations designated by the Director of Banking. Incorporators are also required publish in a CNMI newspaper of general circulation notice of the application.

☐ 3. Apply for Banking License

After the charter is approved by the Director of Banking, incorporators may file:

Name of License	License Fee	Required with application
☐ **Banking License** *Businesses engaged in banking and insurance activities must obtain the license and authority to operate in the CNMI from the Department of Commerce's Banking and Insurance Division.* Banks must report to the Director any significant events (i.e. mergers, stock ownership changes of five percent (5%) or more).	•$5,000 non-refundable application fee •$1,000 license fee • The Banking License may be renewed annually for a fee of one thousand dollars ($1,000).	• Application for Banking License, along with • Current Annual Report • Corporate Charter • Certif of Incorporation/Certificate of Authority • Articles of Incorporation & By-laws • Corporate Stock Register • Corporate Minutes • FDIC Certificate of Membership ***Deposit Insurance Requirement*** Except for banks operating with at least fifty (50) depositors and borrowers as of February 6, 1984, and banks able to demonstrate, upon independent and verifiable authentication, that it has assets in excess of one hundred billion dollars retail banks must obtain insurance of its deposits from the Federal Reserve's Federal Deposit Insurance Corp. ***Capital Requirement*** Banks must maintain, at all times, paid-in cash capital of five hundred thousand dollars ($500,000). Organizational expenses may be counted as part of this capital requirement. ***Reporting Requirements*** The Director of Banking may, at any time, examine the condition of any bank. Banks, therefore, must submit quarterly statements of condition thirty (30) days following the quarter ended (Jan 30, April 30, July 30, and Oct 30). Banks, in addition, must submit to the Director audited financial statements. Documents must be signed by the bank's chief financial officer and certified to be true and correct and in accordance with generally accepted accounting principles by a firm of independent certified public accountants. • Banks must also report to the Director any significant events *(i.e. mergers, stock ownership changes of 5% or more).*

Other Banking -related Licenses

Name of License	License Fee	Required with application
☐ **Finance Co. or Non-Bank Lender License** *Businesses other than banks that provide financing must first obtain a Finance Company or Non-Bank Lender License from the Banking Section.*	Renewed annually for a fee of three hundred dollars ($300).	• *Certif of Incorporation/Cert of Authority* • *Articles of Incorporation* • *By-laws* • *Financial and Income Tax Statements* • *Pro-forma Financial Statements* • *Proposed Loan Documents* • *Resume of Manager, Directors, Officers*
☐ **Foreign Currency Exchange License** *To engage in the business of buying and selling foreign exchange, businesses must first obtain a Foreign Currency (FX) Dealer License from the Banking Section. All FX dealers must appoint an agent.*	The annual license fee for FX dealers is three hundred dollars ($300) while that for agents is thirty dollars ($30).	• Application for Certification of Fitness and Taxicab Operator's ID Card. • Criminal Record Search • Traffic Record Search • Copy of Passport and/or Birth Certificate • Valid CNMI Driver's License • Three (3) 2" x 2" photos • Health Certificate • Sketch of Location • Copy of Bureau of Motor Vehicles Taxi • Operator's License • Receipt of Payment for ID card - $15.00
☐ **Remittance Dealer License** *To engage in the business of receiving money for the purpose of sending it to another country, businesses must first obtain a Remittance Dealer License from the Banking Section.*	The annual fee for a Remittance Dealer License is three hundred dollars ($300) and thirty dollars ($30) for a Remittance Agent License	There is a fifty thousand dollar ($50,000) security deposit requirement to obtain this license. An insurance bond may be substituted for the cash requirement. Those accepting remittance transactions must be licensed as Remittance Agents.

☐ **Investment Company/ Broker-Dealer or Advisor/ Agent License** *Prior to providing investment advice or services in the CNMI, a company or individual must first obtain a license from the Director of Banking. Investment companies and/or agents must show proof of registration with the Securities Exchange Commission and the National Association of Securities Dealers.*	The fee for the Investment Company/ Broker-Dealer License is three hundred dollars ($300) while that for the Investment Advisor /Agent License is fifty dollars ($50).	

*See also: Special Requirements for All Bankers and Insurers

Insurance Licenses
Pre-application Procedure

*See also: Special Requirements for All Bankers and Insurers

☐ 1. Obtain Certificate of Authority

To file for a Certificate of Authority, a completed Application for Certificate of Authority must be submitted to the Insurance Commissioner along with:

- A copy of Annual Statement as of the 31st of December of the prior year
- If a foreign insurer or a domestic reciprocal insurer, an Agreement and Power of Attorney appointing the Insurance Commissioner as its attorney to receive service of legal process. Attach to the Agreement and Power of Attorney a certified copy of a resolution adopted by the insurer's board of directors consenting to the appointment of the Insurance Commissioner to receive service of legal process.
- If a foreign or alien insurer, an Agreement and Power of Attorney appointing a resident agent to receive service of legal process. The general agent must be authorized to appoint subagents and solicitors. For alien insurers, this general agent must also be authorized to countersign on all policies.
- If an alien insurer, a copy of the appointment and authority of its U. S. manager, certified by its proper officer
- If a foreign or alien insurer, a certificate from the public official of its state or country of domicile showing that it is duly organized and is authorized to transact the classes of insurance proposed to be transacted
- An Affidavit of Compliance with the Commonwealth Insurance Act of 1983
- Certificate from proper official of security deposit
- Copy of report of the last examination made of the insurer certified by the insurance supervisory official of its state of domicile or entry into the U.S.
- Other documents or stipulations as the commissioner may require
- Payment fee of three hundred dollars ($300) for a Certificate of Authority
- Articles of Incorporation and By-laws (for review)
- Copy of applicant's rate schedules or rate plans to be used in the CNMI
- Two (2) specimen copies of each policy form to be used in the CNMI. All policies and provisions shall be printed in a type of which the face is not smaller than two-points. Evidence of domiciliary state's approval is required.
- Original Certificate of Good Standing from the state of domicile

☐ 2. Register the Corporation

Within ninety (90) days of the granting of the Certificate of Authority, the insurer must register the corporation with the Registrar of Corporations. The Registrar of Corporations will require evidence of payment of the filing fee of one hundred dollars ($100) with the CNMI Treasury.

□ 3. Apply for Insurance License

Name of License	License Fee	Required with application
□ **Insurance License** *After obtaining a Certificate of Authority, the general agent must submit to the Office of the Insurance Commissioner an Application for Insurance License.*	$75 *Valid for one (1) year and may be renewed annually.*	The application must be accompanied by an Appointment of General Agent form which authorizes the Insurance Commissioner to appoint sub-agents and solicitors, accept service of legal process, and countersign insurance policies.
□ **Sub-agent, Broker, Surplus Lines Broker and Adjuster Licenses** *The Insurance Section also licenses sub-agents (appointed by general agent), brokers, surplus lines brokers, and adjusters.*	$100 each Sub-agent: $75 *Valid for one (1) year and may be renewed annually.*	
□ **Solicitor License** *The application for solicitors or persons that sell insurance and collect premiums is different from that for general agents, sub-agents, brokers, surplus lines brokers, and adjusters.*	$50 *Valid for one (1) year and may be renewed annually.*	A completed Application for Solicitor License must be submitted with • Appointment of Solicitor certificate.

Special Requirements for All Bankers and Insurers

☐ Capital Requirements for Domestic and Alien Insurers

All Insurers Except Life Insurers: All domestic insurers must have a minimum paid-in capital of twenty-five thousand dollars ($25,000) for the transaction of any one (1) class of insurance authorized other than life insurance. For each additional class of insurance to be transacted other than life insurance, there must be an additional paid-in capital of fifteen thousand dollars ($15,000). Insurers having paid-in capital of one hundred thousand dollars ($100,000) may transact any or all classes of insurance authorized, except life insurance. The paid-in capital requirement must be paid in cash.

Life Insurers: Domestic insurers proposing to transact or transacting life insurance must have a minimum paid-in capital of one hundred thousand dollars ($100,000) in addition to the minimum paid-in capital required for other classes of insurance. As with all other insurers, the paid-in capital requirement must be paid in cash.

☐ Reserve Requirements for Life Insurers

All domestic life insurers authorized to transact life insurance must keep and maintain minimum reserves for its life policies based upon Standard Ordinary Mortality Tables acceptable to the Insurance Commissioner and interest at three and a half percent (3.5%) per annum. The minimum reserve requirement must be maintained and kept on deposit in any bank(s) or other financial institution(s) in the CNMI approved by the Insurance Commissioner. Deposits must be legal money of the United States or allowable investment securities, or any combination of such money and securities.

☐ Mandatory Participation in Assigned Risk Plan

CNMI Public Law 11-55 requires all motor vehicle insurance providers to participate in the Assigned Risk Plan (ARP). The Assigned Risk Plan provides minimum motor vehicle liability insurance to persons or parties unable to obtain such coverage. Participating insurance providers are called by the Insurance Commissioner to provide persons or parties applying under the Plan with the minimum coverage. Insurance providers must complete the Application for Insurance Provider License and pay the $250 fee to be part of the ARP.

☐ Reporting Requirements

All insurers must submit on or before April 1 annual financial statements, a form approved by the National Association of Insurance Commissioners, as of the 31st day of December of the prior year.

For more information on obtaining a Banking or an Insurance License, contact:

Banking and Insurance Division,
CNMI Department of Commerce
Caller Box 10007
Capitol Hill, Saipan, MP 96950
Tel.: (670) 664-3008-Saipan; 532-9478-Rota; 433-0853-Tinian
Fax: (670) 664-3067-Saipan; 532-9510-Rota; 433-0678-Tinian
Website: www.commerce.gov.mp

Business Registration, Licensing and Compliance

Applications and Instructions Mentioned in This section That You May Need

Tip: Print this list, ☑ check all that apply and carry with you

- ☐ Partnership Registration Form
- ☐ Annual Partnership Statement
- ☐ Application for Certificate of Authority
- ☐ Certificate of Authority
- ☐ Checklist (for Registration of Domestic Corporations)
- ☐ Certificate of Incorporation
- ☐ Consent and Authorization to Appointment as Registered Agent
- ☐ Annual Corporation Report
- ☐ Application for Amended Certificate of Authority
- ☐ Application for Amended Certificate of Incorporation
- ☐ Application for Reinstatement of Revoked Corporation
- ☐ Application for Reinstatement of a Corporation Administratively Dissolved
- ☐ Certificate of Compliance
- ☐ Application for Certificate of Withdrawal
- ☐ Application for Certificate of Authority - Foreign Limited Liability Company
- ☐ Application for Business License
- ☐ Application for Letter of Compliance and/or Tax Clearance
- ☐ Workers' Compensation Certificate of Clearance
- ☐ Alcoholic Beverage Control License Application
- ☐ Alcoholic Beverage Control License Application - Exhibit "A"
- ☐ Class 3 Retail Dealer's On-Sale General Registration Form
- ☐ Applicant's Business Location/Site Drawing
- ☐ Alcoholic Bev Control Renewal License Instructions (New Applications)
- ☐ Renewal of Alcoholic Beverage Control License (Instructions)
- ☐ List of Employees
- ☐ Application for Tobacco Control License

- ☐ Application for Tobacco Control License (Instructions)
- ☐ Application for Charter of a Commonwealth Bank
- ☐ Application for Banking License
- ☐ Application for Certificate of Authority
- ☐ Agreement and Power of Attorney
- ☐ Affidavit of Compliance
- ☐ Application for Insurance License
- ☐ Appointment of General Agent
- ☐ Application for Solicitor License
- ☐ Appointment of Solicitor
- ☐ Application for Insurance Provider License
- ☐ Food Handler's Certificate Application
- ☐ Food Handler Screening Examination (Report)
- ☐ Temporary Food Handler Certificate
- ☐ Certificate of Completion for Workshop Participation
- ☐ Food Handler Certificate
- ☐ Application for (Nursing) License
- ☐ Application for Certification of Fitness & Taxicab Operator's ID Card
- ☐ Application for Certification of Fitness & Taxicab Operator's ID Card (New)
- ☐ Overview and Requirements
- ☐ Taxicab Vehicle Application
- ☐ Taxicab Vehicle Application Procedure Overview and Requirements
- ☐ Taxicab Vehicle Application Required Documents and Associated Costs

IMPORTANT: See also Chapter 6: Your Physical Location for environmental impact permits you may need for your business operations.

Chapter 5:

LOANS & TAXES ON SAIPAN

This section provides a general summary of CNMI taxes including employees' payroll and income taxes. Individuals, businesses or organizations are urged to consult with the Department of Finance's Division of Revenue and Taxation or other tax authority for specific information or other tax advice. One or more of the following tax types may apply to your business.

Bank Loans

Getting Loans, Financial Assistance

Aside from personal savings or loans from family, friends, or investors, banks are the most common source of financing for businesses.

The private banks currently operating in the CNMI include Bank of Guam, Bank of Hawaii, First Hawaiian Bank, Bank Pacific, Bank of Saipan and City Trust Bank. Each institution has its own specific requirements for qualification and terms for approval. Contact the banks for detailed information on service offerings.

Commonwealth Development Authority

Government Financing

Eligible business may also secure financing from the government. CDA has three (2) loan programs available for businesses establishing, expanding, or modernizing facilities in the CNMI:

- Direct Loan Program
- Loan Guarantee Program

To be eligible to apply under any of CDA's loan programs, applicants must be one of the following:

- Commonwealth citizens
- U.S. citizens or nationals with two years continuous residency in the CNMI
- Partnership or association wholly owned by CNMI citizens
- Corporation organized under the laws of the CNMI with fifty-one percent (51%) capital stock owned by CNMI citizens
- U.S. Corporation, Partnership or Association licensed and registered under the laws of the CNMI actually doing business in the CNMI for at least two (2) years Another prerequisite for obtaining a loan from CDA are three (3) letters of denial from local banks. The denial letters must be for loan applications for the same business purpose and amount being applied for at CDA. CDA is a lender of last resort; the requirement of such letter keeps CDA from competing with local lending institutions.

Direct Loan Program

The Direct Loan Program offers agricultural, marine, and commercial loans to qualified applicants.

The maximum term on direct loans is thirty (30) years. The interest rate on agricultural and marine loans is four and a half percent (4.5%), fixed, while the rate on commercial loans is seven percent (7%), fixed.

Loan Guarantee Program

CDA leverages its limited resources by soliciting the participation of commercial lending institutions in funding business ventures for local entrepreneurs. Under the guarantee program, the bank approves and disburses the loan which CDA can guarantee up to ninety percent (90%) of the total term loan or revolving line of credit. The banks that are currently doing business with CDA are Bank of Guam, Bank of Hawaii, and Bank of Saipan.

The maximum term on loan guarantees is twenty (20) years. Interest rates are set at the bank's prevailing rate. Guaranteed loans and revolving lines of credit facilities are evaluated and must meet the same underwriting criteria and eligibility requirements as direct loans with CDA.

Persons interested in any of CDA's financing options must submit the CDA Loan Application along with the following:

- Business plan
- Land documents (Land title)
- Property map, if surveyed by a Certified Surveyor
- Specific Use of Fund Statement
- Declination letter from at three (3) banks on the proposed project
- Financial Statements for last two (2) years, if applicable
- List of Collateral being offered
- Project Income and Expenses for one (1) year
- Personal Financial Statement for each applicant
- Resume
- Authorization form to obtain credit information
- Payment of credit report fee of ten dollars ($10) per applicant
- Tax Compliance from the Division of Revenue and Taxation
- If a corporation, Corporate Resolution to Borrow, Articles of Incorporation, By-laws, Annual Report and Certification from the Registrar of Corporations that Corporation is in good order
- If a partnership, Partnership Agreement
- Personnel requirement for proposed project

Other Sources Of Financing

There are unique grants and loans which may be available to do research, start businesses and grow existing ventures. As a territory of the United States, the CNMI and businesses started here are in a unique position to qualify for special monies.

Visit CCR Website and become a registered vendor

Visit www.Grants.gov

Visit Dept of Energy website

The U.S. Department of Agriculture and the U.S. Department of Energy recently announced a combined total of up to $18 million will be available for research and development of biomass-based products, biofuels, bioenergy and related processes.

For more details on the types of financing options available or application requirements, contact:

Commonwealth Development Authority
P.O. Box 502149
Wakin's Building
Gualo Rai, Saipan, MP 96950
Tel.: (670) 234-6245/6293/7145-Saipan;
532-9408-Rota;
433-9203-Tinian

Fax: (670) 234-7144 or 235-7147-Saipan;
532-9407-Rota;
433-3690-Tinian
E-mail: administration@cda.gov.mp
Website: www.cda.gov.mp

CNMI and Federal Taxes

☐ Northern Marianas Territorial Income Tax (NMTIT)

The NMTIT mirrors U.S. Internal Revenue Code except where incompatible with the Covenant to Establish a Commonwealth of the Northern Mariana Islands in Political Union with the US or CNMI tax laws.

Sole proprietorships, partnerships, corporations and other taxable entities must report and pay income taxes on CNMI-sourced income. The NMTIT is assessed at graduated rates. Rate tables may be obtained from the Division of Revenue and Taxation or from the U.S. Internal Revenue Service's (IRS's) Publication 15, Circular E, Employer's Tax Guide.

Pursuant to the Covenant and CNMI tax laws, taxable entities subject to the NMTIT are entitled to a rebate on their NMTIT tax liability. The rebate ranges from fifty to ninety (50-90%) depending on the amount of tax paid.

Northern Marianas Territorial Income Tax (NMTIT) Rebate Amounts for Corporate and Non-Corporate Taxpayers	
Income	Rebate
Less than $20,000	90%
$20,001 - $100,000	$18,000 + 70% of amount over $20,000
Greater than $100,000	$74,000 + 50% of amount over $150,000

Source: Division of Revenue & Taxation

☐ Earnings Tax

Earnings from sources within the CNMI not derived from employment or business are subject to the Earnings Tax. The Earnings Tax is applicable to gains from the sale or lease of personal property and winnings from gambling, lottery, raffle or other similar activities. Any Earnings Tax paid is allowed as a non-refundable credit against the NMTIT.

Earnings Tax	
$0 - $1,000	0
$1,001 - $5,000	2%
$5,001 - $7,000	3%
$7,001 - $15,000	4%
$15,001 - $22,000	5%
$22,001 - $30,000	6%
$30,001 - $40,000	7%
$40,001 - $50,000	8%
Over $50,000	9%

Source: Division of Revenue & Taxation

☐ Business Gross Revenue Tax (Bgrt)

Business gross revenues sourced within the CNMI are subject to the Business Gross Revenue Tax (BGRT). BGRT taxes must be paid on a quarterly basis. Returns are due on or before the last day of the month following the end of the quarter. Special rates apply to agricultural producers, fisheries, manufacturers, wholesalers, and financial institutions. Manufacturers that export products from the CNMI are exempt from the BGRT.

Annual Gross Revenues Tax	
Annual Gross Revenue	Tax Rate
$0 - $5,000	No tax
$5,001 - $50,000	1.5%
$50,001 - $100,000	2.0%
$100,001 - $250,000	2.5%
$250,001 - $500,000	3%
$500,001 - $750,000	4%
Over $750,000	5%

Source: Division of Revenue & Taxation

SPECIAL Business Gross Revenues Tax	
Industry	Tax Rate
Agricultural Producers & Fisheries	$0 if annual gross revenue is $0 - $20,000 1% of annual gross revenue if annual gross revenue is > $20,000
Manufacturers & Wholesalers	$0 if annual gross revenue is $0 - $5,000 1.5% of annual gross revenue if annual gross revenue is $5,001 - $50,000 2% of annual gross revenue if annual gross revenue is > $50,000
Financial Institutions	Pay the greater of 5% of net income OR 3% of gross revenue

Source: Division of Revenue & Taxation

☐ General Excise Tax

Goods imported into the CNMI for business purposes or for personal use exceeding the amount allowed under the law are subject to the General Excise Tax. The General Excise Tax rate varies for each type of commodity. The General Excise Tax is collected by the Division of Customs at ports of entry. Rates are given below

General Excise Tax Rates	
Agricultural products	1% ad valorem
Beer and malt beverages	$0.02/oz
Boats/yachts not exceeding $500,000	5% ad valorem
Cigarettes	$1.75/20 cigarettes
CNMI produced goods	1% of retail price
Construction equipment, materials and machinery	3% ad valorem
Cosmetics	17.25% ad valorem
Distilled alcoholic beverages	$.18/oz.
Food stuffs	1% ad valorem
Hygiene products	1% ad valorem
Jewelry	5.75% ad valorem
Leather	goods 5.75% ad valorem
Luxury boats/yachts in excess of $500,000	5.75% ad valorem
Luxury passenger vehicles in excess of $30,000	5.75% ad valorem
Passenger vehicles not exceeding $30,000	5% ad valorem
Perfumes	23% ad valorem
Precious metals/stones	5.75% ad valorem
Prescription drugs and medicines	1% ad valorem
Soft drinks	$.06/12 oz.
Tobacco products	60% invoice price
Wine and sake	$.05/oz.
All others	5% ad valorem

ad valorem: According to value. A tax, duty, or fee which varies based on the value of the products, services, or property on which it is levied. The term **ad valorem** is derived from the Latin **ad** valentiam, meaning "to the value."

☐ Environmental Beautification Tax

CNMI Public Law 13-42 recently established the Environmental Beautification Tax to be assessed on all imported consumer goods . The tax is set at the rate of .42 percent ad valorem and is collected by the Division of Customs at ports of entry.

☐ Fuel Tax

Sellers and distributors of liquid and aviation fuel are subject to fuel taxes. The rate for liquid fuel is fifteen cents ($.15) per gallon while that for aviation fuel is three percent (3%) ad valorem. This fuel tax does not apply to sales of liquid fuel to the Commonwealth Utilities Corporation with certain provisions. The Fuel Tax is assessed and collected by the Division of Customs at ports of entry.

☐ Beverage Container Tax

Soft drink and alcoholic beverage containers are subject to the Beverage Container Tax. A tax of five cents ($.05) is imposed on soft drink and alcoholic beverage containers. The Beverage Container Tax is assessed and collected by the Division of Customs at ports of entry.

☐ User Fee

Persons or businesses requiring certification from the Department of Finance for country of origin or other purposes relating to CNMI are assessed a user fee. The user fee is three and seven-tenths of a percent (3.7%) of the gross value of the merchandise to be certified. This fee is due and payable to the Commonwealth Treasury upon certification.

As with the General Excise, Environmental Beautification, Fuel , Beverage Container taxes, the user fee is assessed and collected by the Division of Customs.

☐ Alcoholic Beverage/Bar Tax

Businesses licensed to serve alcoholic beverages for consumption on the premises of the establishment are assessed a tax of ten percent (10%) of the total charge for any alcoholic beverage sold or consumed at the establishment. The Alcoholic Beverage/ Bar Tax must be filed with the Division of Revenue and Taxation on a monthly basis and paid before the twentieth (20th) day of the succeeding month.

☐ Hotel Occupancy Tax

Transient occupants of a room or rooms in a hotel, lodging house, or similar facility in the CNMI are assessed an occupancy tax of ten percent (10%) of the amount charged or paid for the accommodations. The person who operates owns or manages a hotel, lodging house or similar facility is responsible for collecting the tax. The tax must be collected at the time rent is paid or charged. The tax must be reported and remitted to the Division of Revenue and Taxation before the twentieth (20th) day of the succeeding month.

☐ Gaming Machine Jackpot Tax

A tax of twenty percent (20%) is assessed on all jackpot winnings from poker machines, pachinko machines, slot machines, pachinko slot machines, and similar gaming devices. Game room establishments are responsible for collecting the tax and keeping all records, and may be held liable for uncollected taxes.

☐ Entities Exempt From Paying CNMI Taxes

Non-profit organizations are subject to applicable CNMI taxes unless the organization applies for and is granted tax-exempt status by the Division of Revenue and Taxation. Organizations granted tax-exempt status are not exempt from taxation on taxable income from unrelated business activities.

Foreign sales corporations (FSCs) are exempt from the BGRT and NMTIT. In order to qualify for such tax exemptions, FSCs must apply for an FSC license with the Secretary of Finance. All FSC license applications must submitted with the following: a) a copy of the company's articles of incorporation and bylaws; b) a copy of its most recent election to be treated as an FSC or, if it has not yet made an election, a pledge to furnish the Secretary of Finance a copy of its election within ninety (90) days after making the election; c) information on its resident director and the location of its Commonwealth office; and d) its $500 license fee.

Although exempt from the BGRT and NMTIT, foreign sales corporations must file informational tax returns with the Division of Revenue and Taxation. Informational returns must be submitted along with schedules and worksheets at the same time the FSC's tax returns are filed with the U.S. Internal Revenue Service. The Division of Revenue and Taxation may require additional information substantiating qualifications for foreign sales corporation treatment under the U.S. Internal Revenue Code.

Employment Taxes

Employers are responsible for the timely filing of employees' withheld CNMI and federal income taxes and payroll taxes. Because of the complex nature of income and payroll taxes, it is highly recommended that businesses consult with or retain the services of certified public accountants or reputable accounting firms. Look in the Yellow Pages for a listing of accountants and accounting firms.

This section summarizes CNMI and federal requirements for employee income tax withholding and payroll tax payment.

Employment Tax

Companies with employees must have each employee complete a

☐ Form W-4, Employee's Withholding Allowance Certificate.

Form W-4, the Employee's Withholding Allowance Certificate, is used to determine how much income tax to withhold from employees' wages.

Employers file

☐ Form W-2, Wage and Tax Statement,

to report wages paid to each employee from whom Income, Social Security, or Medicare taxes were withheld or Income tax would have been withheld if the employee had claimed no more than one withholding allowance or had not claimed exemption from withholding on Form W-4, Employee's Withholding Allowance Certificate. Employers file

☐ Form W-3, Transmittal of Wage and Tax Statements,

to transmit Copy A of Form W-2, Wage and Tax Statement. Employers must submit Copy A to the Social Security Administration by the last day in February (or on the following workday if this date falls on a Saturday, Sunday or holiday), for the previous year. Copies B and C are furnished to the employee by January 31 (or on following workday if this date falls on a Saturday, Sunday or holiday. Copy B must accompany the employee's income tax return and Copy C is the employee's copy. Employers retain Copy D for four years for records purposes.

Employers are responsible for depositing employees' withheld income and payroll taxes with the Div of Revenue & Taxation. These withholdings payments must be remitted to the Division of Revenue and Taxation on the following form:

☐ Deposit Form 500-WH.

The filing schedule varies, depending on the amount of tax liability. Employers should contact the Division of Revenue and Taxation or other tax authority to ascertain the filing schedule for the business.

☐ Wage and Salary Tax (WST)

EMPLOYEE PAYS; EMPLOYER WITHHOLDS. In addition to the NMTIT, an annual tax is imposed on all wages and salaries from sources within the CNMI. As with the NMTIT, the employer withholds the WST and remits it to the Division of Revenue and Taxation on behalf of the employee.

Wage and Salary Tax	
Annual Gross Wages	Tax Rate
$0 - $1,000	No tax
$1,001 - $5,000	2%
$5,001 - $7,000	3%
$7,001 - $15,000	4%
$15,001 - $22,000	5%
$22,001 - $30,000	6%
$30,001 - $40,000	7%
$40,001 - $50,000	8%
Over $50,000	9%

Source: Division of Revenue & Taxation

Generally, any WST paid on wages sourced within the CNMI is allowed as a non-refundable credit against the NMTIT. For more information on the NMTIT and WST taxes, contact:

Division of Revenue and Taxation
CNMI Department of Finance
P.O. Box 5234 CHRB
1st Floor, Joeten Commercial Building
Dandan, Saipan, MP 96950
Tel.: (670) 664-1000-Saipan; 532-1040-Rota; 433-1600-Tinian
Fax: (670) 664-1015-Saipan; 532-0473-Rota; 433-1615-Tinian

US Federal Government Employment Taxes

☐ Federal Insurance Contributions Act (FICA)

EMPLOYER WITHHOLDS AND EMPLOYER MATCHES. The FICA establishes a system of old-age, survivors, disability, and hospital insurance. The FICA consists of the Social Security tax and the Medicare tax. The Social Security tax finances the old-age, survivors, and disability insurance portion while the Medicare tax subsidizes the hospital insurance portion.

Employers withhold the Social Security and Medicare taxes for the employee; employers also make matching tax payments of the same amounts to the IRS. The Social Security tax applies to wages up to a maximum wage base. The Medicare tax, on the other hand, applies to all wages with no maximum wage base.

The current wage base limit and tax rates may be obtained from Publication 15, Circular E, Employer's Tax Guide. The Social Security rate for 2003 is six and two-tenths of a percent (6.2%) with a maximum wage base of eighty-seven thousand dollars ($87,000). This maximum wage base on which Social Security taxes are paid is indexed to inflation and changes annually. New maximum wage base amounts are usually announced in November. Unlike the Social Security tax, the Medicare tax has no wage base limit. The Medicare tax rate for 2003 is 1.45%.

FICA tax rates are summarized below. Sole proprietorships or self-employed individuals pay both the employer and employee portions of the Social Security and Medicare taxes.

FICA tax payments are made either monthly or semi-weekly depending on the amount owed during a four-quarter look-back period. Payments may be made electronically using the Electronic Federal Tax Payment System (EFTPS).

Federal Insurance Contributions Act (FICA) Tax Rates

Tax	Rate
Social Security Tax	
Employee	6.2% on first $87,000 of wages
Employer	6.2% on first $87,000 of wages
Self-employed	12.4% on first $87,000 of net earnings
Medicare Tax	
Employee	1.45% on all wages
Employer	1.45% on all wages
Self-employed	2.9% on net earnings

Source: Publication 15, Circular E, Employer's Tax Guide; Internal Revenue Service

To enroll in EFTPS, visit www.eftps.gov or call (800) 945-8400 or (800) 555-4477. Payments may also be made by delivering

☐ Form 8109, Federal Tax Deposit Coupon,

with payment to an institution authorized to accept federal tax deposits, or mailing directly to:

Internal Revenue Service
Philadelphia, PA 19255-0215

For information on when tax deposits are due to the federal government or for any other information related to the FICA tax, contact:

Internal Revenue Service
Toll free: (800) 829-1040
Tel: (216) 516-2000 - (Mon-Fri; 6:00 a.m. - 2:00 a.m. EST)
Fax: (215) 516-2555

For more information or instructions on reporting Social Security and Medicare taxes, contact:

Social Security Administration
2nd Floor, Marina Heights II Building
Puerto Rico, Saipan, MP 96950
Tel.: (670) 234-6683-Saipan; 532-9421-Rota; 433-9421-Tinian
Fax: (670) 234-3022-Saipan
Website: www.ssa.gov/employer/

CNMI Tax Compliance
Applications and Instructions Mentioned in Chapter 5 That You May Need

Tip: Print this list, ☑ check all that apply and carry with you

- ☐ CDA Loan Application
- ☐ IRS Form W-7, Application for IRS Individual. Taxpayer ID Number
- ☐ Form SS-5, Application for A Social Security Card
- ☐ Publication 15, Circular E, Employer's Tax Guide
- ☐ CNMI Workers' Compensation Tariff and Underwriting Manual
- ☐ Workers' Compensation Certificate of Clearance
- ☐ Notice of Insurance Coverage
- ☐ Form W-4, Employee's Withholding Allowance Certificate
- ☐ Form W-2, Wage and Tax Statement
- ☐ Form W-3, Transmittal of Wage and Tax Statements
- ☐ Deposit Form 500-WH
- ☐ Form 8109, Federal Tax Deposit Coupon

For more information on the CNMI tax system, contact:

Division of Revenue and Taxation
CNMI Department of Finance
P.O. Box 5234 CHRB
1st Floor, Joeten Commercial Building
Dandan, Saipan, MP 96950
Tel.: (670) 664-1000-Saipan; 532-1040-Rota; 433-1600-Tinian
Fax: (670) 664-1015-Saipan; 532-0473-Rota; 433-1615-Tinian

For information on the General Excise, Fuel, Environmental Beautification, and Beverage Container taxes or the User Fee, contact:

Division of Customs
CNMI Department of Finance
P.O. Box 5234 CHRB
Puerto Rico, Saipan, MP 96950
Tel.: (670) 664-1601-Saipan; 532-9455-Rota; 433-1600-Tinian
Fax: (670) 664-1615-Saipan; 532-0473-Rota; 433-1615-Tinian

Chapter 6: Your Physical Location

Zoning Approval
Finding a Location
Building Permits and Compliance
Environmental Impact and Permits
Utilities
Phone Service
Hiring Employees

Finding a Location

• To find little-known space for rent on Saipan, Tinian and Rota, contact the Commonwealth Development Authority. This office is in possession of foreclosed and defaulted property, and has information on property owners who are "motivated" sellers and renters.

• To find property for rent or lease, as well as a range of items, visit garagesale.saipan.com

• A list of real estate firms may be found in the Yellow Pages of local telephone and business directories.

Leasing Land

At present, only persons of CNMI descent may own land in the CNMI. Non-indigenous persons, however, may lease private land for up to fifty-five (55) years. Numerous private firms offer assistance in locating real property. Individuals or parties interested in leasing land are advised to consult with a reputable real estate agent and a CNMI licensed attorney. Land transactions require numerous checks such as confirming with the Commonwealth Land Commission and Recorder's Office rightful ownership of the property being negotiated, ascertaining that lease documents are properly filed, etc.

Public land is also available for lease if private land cannot be identified and secured for a project or development. The Marianas Public Lands Authority is the agency responsible for administering public land leases. Under the law, public land may be leased for up to twenty-five (25) years. Lease extensions of not more than fifteen (15) years may be granted with approval by three-fourths (3/4) of the members of the CNMI Legislature. Leases of more than five (5) hectares of public land for commercial use purposes must be approved by a majority of members of the Legislature.

To lease public land, the Marianas Public Lands Authority requires:

1.Statement indicating that no property is available for the proposed project after two weeks of advertisement in a local newspaper or radio station.

2.General background data of the applicant, including:
   a. Personal data of officials or owners of the company, including:
      i. Work Experiences
      ii. Police Clearance for past ten (10) years from country of origin

b. Overall Description of Company
   i. Type(s) of Business
   ii. Corporate Documents
   iii. Organizational Structure
   iv. Business License

3.Development and Operating Plans
   a. Purpose of Lease
   b. Description of site needed for the project
   c. Schematic plan of the development to be constructed on the site
   d. Operating plan with general description of each component including equipment inventory and manpower requirement

4.Financial Statements
   a. Funding source for the investment
   b. Cost of investment in detail
   c. Financial projection for the first five (5) years of operation of business

5.Non-refundable application fee of five thousand dollars ($5,000) payable in full upon submission of application

6.Certification that all statements made in the application are true and correct under penalty of perjury

7.Certification authorizing the Marianas Public Lands Authority to conduct investigation into financial status of applicant and business officers

For more information on the leasing of government land, contact:

Department of Public Lands
P.O. Box 500380
2nd Floor, Joeten Commercial Center
Dandan, Saipan, MP 96950
Saipan: (670) 234-3751/3752/3757
Rota: 532-9431; Tinian; 433-9245
Fax: (670) 234-3755-Saipan; 532-9430-Rota; 433-0599-Tinian

Zoning , Part 2 (Approval)

Quite simply, in order to obtain Zoning Board approval, your proposed business location must be "zoned" for the type of business you wish to operate. If you are proposing a new establishment, you must also provide certain drawings and documents to ensure that the structure you build conforms to certain zoning, frontage, signage, parking requirements.

The Zoning Law of 2008 document available at zoning.gov.mp is very thorough and provides definitions, sample drawings, maps and charts for determining zoning compliance. There's no substitute for an actual review of the Zoning Law, but here are a few of the frequently asked questions

Bed and Breakfast

1. Can a leaseholder have a bed & breakfast in their home? **Possibly. See Guidelines.**

Home Business

1. I am opening a business in my home. Do I need a zoning permit? **A: YES**
2. I am babysitting children in my home for free. Do I need a zoning permit? **A: NO**
3. I am babysitting children in my home and being paid by the government. Do I need a zoning permit? **A: Yes. You are operating a business and need a zoning permit.**

Massage Parlor

1. The Zoning Law says a massage parlor located in a hotel with more than 20 rooms is not considered as an adult business (Section 103, Definition of "Massage Parlor"). Does the massage parlor have to be inside the hotel? **See Zoning Guidelines.**

Nonconforming Use or Structure

1. I have a building that has been vacant for more than six months but the kind of use I want to do there isn't allowed under the Zoning Law. What can I do? **A: You should discuss this with the Zoning Office. Consider applying for a rezone.**

Opening or Moving a Business

1. I am opening a business in Chalan Kanoa, and a branch in Garapan. My business is permitted in both districts. Do I apply separately and do I pay twice? **A: A zoning permit and application fee is needed for each location.**

2. I am changing the location of the business to a zoning district that allows my use. Do I pay a fee? **A: You need a zoning permit and pay a fee if you are opening a business that is new to Saipan or moving a business from one location to another.**

3. I am buying an existing business. Do I need zoning permit? **A: You do not need a zoning permit just to transfer ownership or to renew a business license. The Zoning Office can give you a form to take to the Business License office.**

4. What do I do when I want to set up a business, such as retail or restaurant, on my own property and the business is not permitted in my area? **A: You may not open a business that is not permitted.**

5. We are going to rent a space in the XYZ building but the owner is not on island. Can I still submit this application? **A: If the owner designates an agent, the agent may submit the application on behalf of the owner.**

6. I have a client who is registering a new business on Saipan but she doesn't yet have a business location and is using my address temporarily. Do I still need to submit a zoning application? **A: Your client does not need to submit a zoning application if they are only using your address for registration or mailing address purposes. Your client will need to apply for a zoning permit when she starts doing business.**

Permits, Processing, Fees

1. How much is the fee for a Zoning Inquiry? **None**

2. Is it okay to call for follow-up of our application?
Yes, but don't call every day. We will call you whenyour permit is ready for pickup.

3. How many days does it take for a permit to be issued?
This depends on our workload and the complexity of the permit. Most permits are issued within 2-3 weeks.

4. Can I pay the zoning fee together with my business license fee?
You can pay at the same location but the payments go to separate accounts.

5. Do I need to pay separate fee for sign on top of fee for my new business?
A: You may combine your sign application with another zoning permit application and just pay one fee.

6. If I designate x as my agent, can x sign the permit on my behalf? **A: YES**

Signs

1. Can I put a public service sign in the road right-of-way?
A: The only signs allowed in the right-of-way are "traffic signs" regulating the flow of traffic. A public service sign may be considered to be a traffic sign if the approved as such by DPW.

Single Family Home

1. I am building or remodeling my single family home. Do I need zoning approval?
You do not need zoning approval but there are zoning standards that apply to your development. You should consult the Zoning Law or contact the Zoning Office. Also see Zoning Guideline 2008-04.

Temporary Permits

1. How long is a temporary permit good for?
Temporary permits may be issued for up to six months.

Building Permits and Compliance

Complying With The Building Safety Code

The CNMI Building Safety Code ("the Code") was established by Public Law 6-45, and provides standards for the location, design, material, construction, enlargement, maintenance, use, occupancy, and moving of buildings.

Before constructing or renovating a building, installing heating appliances, electrical fixtures or outlets, a building permit must be obtained from the Building Safety Office of the Department of Public Works. The building permit process ensures adequate maintenance of buildings, protection of the health, safety and welfare of people and compliance with applicable regulations.

☐ Secure other permits.

Before applying for a building permit, developers must first secure all other applicable permits from the Division of Environmental Quality, Division of Historical Preservation, Coastal Resources Management, U.S. Army Corps of Engineers, or other federal/local govt agency regulating the particular activity.

☐ Submit Application for Building Permit/Plan Review/Floodplain

Applications for Building Permit/Plan Review/Floodplain must be submitted along with at least two (2) copies of Drawings and Specifications drawn to scale with sufficient clarity and dimensions to show the nature and character of the work to be performed. Should the quality of materials be essential for compliance with the Safety Code, specific information shall be given to establish such quality. The Building Safety Official may waive the requirement for filing drawings if the project involves minor work. Consult with the Building Safety Official for format and size requirements for Drawings and Specifications.

☐ Submit Site Plan

Developers must submit a Site Plan showing the scale, size and location of the new construction and all existing structures on the site and the distance from lot lines and the established street grades. The Site Plan must be drawn in accordance with an accurate boundary line survey. In the case of demolition, the Site Plan must show all construction to be demolished and the location and size of all existing buildings to remain on the site. As with the requirement to file Drawings and Specifications, the Building Safety Official may waive the requirement for filing of Site Plans if the work involved is minor in nature.

☐ Submit Details of all proposed work

Adequate details of structural, mechanical and electrical work including computations, stress diagrams and other technical data are also required at time of filing of the application. Engineering drawings and computations must bear the signature of a CNMI licensed professional engineer or architect.

☐ Provide estimated project cost and evidence of tax credit

Also required for a complete application package is a statement of estimated total project cost and evidence of tax credit. Total project cost includes all costs for architectural and engineering design, professional services, on-site construction materials, and labor including construction management, administration and supervision costs.

☐ Pay Fees

Payment of the applicable Plan-Review Fee, the Building Permit Fee, and other applicable fees must be made to the Building Safety Official before applications are accepted. Upon finding conformity with all building safety requirements and applicable laws, the Building Safety Official will issue the building permit.

Fees

Plan Review Fees		
Building Type	**Construction Cost**	**Fee**
Residential	Greater than $2,000 but less than $50,000	½ of Building Permit Fee
Residential	Greater than $50,000	¾ of Building Permit Fee
Commercial	$1,000 or greater	¾ of Building Permit Fee

Source: Building Safety Division, Department of Public Works

Building Permit Fees	
Construction Cost	**Fee**
$1 to $500	$15
$501 to $2,000	$15 for first $500 plus $2 for each additional $100 or fraction thereof, to and including $2,000
$2,001 to $25,000	$45 for the first $2,000 plus $9 for each additional $1,000 or fraction thereof, to and including $25,000
$25,001 to $50,000	$252 for the first $25,000 plus $7 for each additional $1,000 or fraction thereof, to and including $50,000
$50,001 to $100,000	$427 for the first $50,000 plus $5 for each additional $1,000 or fraction thereof, to and including $100,000
$100,001 to $500,000	$677 for the first $100,000 plus $5 for each additional $1,000 or fraction thereof, to and including $500,000
$500,001 to $1,000,000	$2,677 for the first $500,000 and $3 for each additional $1,000 or fraction thereof, to and including $1,000,000
$1,000,001 or greater	$4,177 for the first $1,000,000 plus $2 for each additional $1,000 or fraction thereof, to and including $1,000,000

Example: If your project is estimated to cost you $63,500, your fee would be (row 5)

$427 First $50,000 (1 x $427)

$65 for each add'l $1,000 (13 x $5)

$5 for fraction of $1,000 (1 x $5)

$497 TOTAL Building Permit Fee

Special Permit Fees	
Type of Permit	Fee
Demolition and Removal Commercial	$150
Demolition and Removal Residential	$75
Grading Plan Review	
50 cubic yards or less	$0
51 to 100 cubic yards	$22.50
101 to 10,000 cubic yards	$30
10,001 to 100,000 cubic yards	30 for the first 10,000 cubic yds plus $15 for each additional 10,000 cubic yds or fraction
100,001 to 200,000 cubic yds	$165 for the first 100,000 cubic yards plus $9 for each additional 10,000 cubic yds or fraction
200,000 cubic yds or more	$255 for the first 200,000 cubic yards plus $4.50 for each additional 10,000 cubic yds or fraction
Grading Permit	
50 cubic yds or less	$15
51 to 100 cubic yds	$22.50
101 to 1,000 cubic yds	$22.50 for the first 100 cubic yds plus $10.50 for each additional 100 cubic yds or fraction thereof
1,001 to 10,000 cubic yds	$117 for the first 1,000 cubic yds plus $9 for each additional 1,000 cubic yds or fraction thereof
10,001 to 100,000 cubic yds	$198 for the first 10,000 cubic yds plus $40.50 for each additional 10,000 cubic yds or fraction
100,001 cubic yds or more	$562.50 for the first 100,000 cubic yds plus $22.50 for each add'l 10,000 cubic yds or fraction
Other Special Fees Building Permits	
Placards and Applications	$20 per copy
Certificate of Occupancy	$15 for original placard
Bld Safety Code, Amendments & Rules/Reg	$13 per copy
Change of Contractor	$20
Schedule of Inspection Request	$10
Photostat Copy of a Plan 18" x 24"	$2.50 per shot
Photostat Copy of a Plan 24" x 36"	$4.00 per shot
Revised Plan	$50 per revision
Reinspection Fees	$45 per hour
Signs	$100
Relocation or Moving	$150
Inspection outside Normal Business Hours	$30 per hour
Reinspection Fees	$30 per hour
Renewal of Permits	75% of amount for new permit provided no changes were made to original plan, and time of suspension or abandonment does not exceed 1 year since the issuance of the original permit
Additional Plan Review Fees	the greater of the following: $30 per hour or the total hourly cost to DPW and/or CNMI gov't including overhead, equipment, hourly wages and fringe benefits of the employees involved

The building permit and approved Drawings and Specifications must be kept at the worksite at all times. Work at the site may begin after the permit holder posts an Inspection Card in a conspicuous place on the premises and in a position to allow the Building Safety Official or his/her authorized representative to make entries. The Inspection Card is issued by the Building Safety Official.

After all required inspections are made and the project is found to be in accordance with all building safety requirements and applicable laws, the Building Safety Official will issue a Certificate of Occupancy. The building can be occupied or used, in whole or in part, only after the Certificate of Occupancy is issued. The Certificate of Occupancy must remain posted indefinitely in a conspicuous place.

☐ The Developer Infrastructure Tax

The Developer Infrastructure Tax is a two percent (2%) tax assessed on the total project cost for new commercial developments. The Building Safety Official reviews all applications to determine if the tax is applicable to the project. CNMI Public Law 8-23, as amended by CNMI Public Law 9-14, exempts:

a) new residential construction with two or fewer dwelling units;

b) alterations or expansion of single family homes or duplexes where no additional units are created and use is not changed;

c) construction of accessory buildings or structures that does not result in additional demand for electricity, water, sewage or solid waste disposal;

d) the replacement of destroyed or partially destroyed multi-family dwellings or commercial buildings or structures that does not result in additional demand for electricity, water, sewage or solid waste disposal;

e) changes in the type of use for a structure or land that does not result in additional demand for electricity, water, sewage or solid waste disposal; and

f) structural developments of non-profit religious and educational organizations for religious and educational purposes.

If applicable to the project, the Building Safety Official will issue the developer a voucher for payment. Developers subject to the tax are also assessed a non-refundable administrative fee equal to the building permit fee. See Table The tax, administrative fee, and all other fees may be deposited or paid at the CNMI Treasury, the Division of Revenue and Taxation, or other authorized collection points.

When a project is completed, the developer submits a statement on actual total project cost including any adjustments for change orders. Developers are liable for the total tax based on this final total project cost less any previous payments or tax credits. The Certificate of Occupancy will not be issued by the Building Safety Official until the total tax is collected.

Flood Hazard Design Requirements

As the administering agency of the CNMI Flood Damage Prevention Program, the Building Safety Office's Flood Plain Administrator will review building permit applications to determine if proposed projects are located within special flood zones.

Projects located in flood-prone areas are required to submit program documents and will be advised of:

1) the availability of federally subsidized flood insurance;
2) eligibility for federal disaster assistance; and
3) flood hazard design requirements.

For more information on building permit application requirements, the developer infrastructure tax, flood hazard design requirements, contact:

Building Safety Division
CNMI Department of Public Works
Caller Box 10007
2nd Floor, Joeten Commercial Building
Gualo Rai, Saipan, MP 96950
Tel.: (670) 235-5827/5828-Saipan; 532-3870-Rota; 433-9255-Tinian
Fax: (670) 235-6346; 532-3099-Rota; 433-9242-Tinian

Complying With Public Accommodations Requirements Of The Americans With Disabilities Act

Title III, Public Accommodations of the Americans with Disabilities Act (ADA) prohibits private entities from discriminating on the basis of disability in places of public accommodation. Title III requires all newly constructed and altered places of public accommodation and commercial facilities to be designed and constructed in such a manner that they are readily accessible to and usable by persons with disabilities.

Title III defines a public accommodation as a private entity that owns, leases, leases to, or operates a place of public accommodation. Title III identifies twelve (12) categories of public accommodation:

1. places of lodging (e.g., hotels, motels);
2. places serving food and drink (e.g., restaurants, bars);
3. places of public entertainment (e.g., movies, theaters, stadiums, concert halls);
4. places of public gathering (e.g., auditoriums, convention centers);
5. sales or rental establishments (e.g. stores);
6. service establishments (gas stations, dry cleaners, banks, doctors, lawyers'
7. transportation stations (e.g., terminals, depots);
8. places of public display or collection (e.g., museums, libraries);
9. places of recreation (e.g., parks, zoos, amusement parks);
10. private schools;
11. social services (day care, food banks, homeless shelters, adoption agencies);
12. places of exercise or recreation (gym, health spas, bowling alleys, golf course)

All entities that fall under any of the above categories have been subject to the nondiscrimination requirements of Title III since January 26, 1992, regardless of the number of employees as such entities. For general guidelines or technical assistance on nondiscrimination requirements of Title III of the ADA, contact:

CNMI Council on Developmental Disabilities
P.O. Box 502565
Capitol Hill, Saipan, MP 96950
Tel. (670) 664-7000; Fax: (670) 664-7030
E-mail: gddc@cnmiddcouncil.org
Website: cnmiddcouncil.org

The information, materials, and/or technical assistance provided by the CNMI Council on Developmental Disabilities are intended solely as informal guidance and are neither a determination of legal rights or responsibilities under the ADA, nor binding on any agency with enforcement responsibility under the ADA. Individuals or businesses should consult with an attorney if legal advise or assistance is required.

Renting Or Leasing An Office Or Facility

Businesses not interested in building a structure or facility may rent or lease space. Rent or lease options provide more choice in location, are more affordable, help free up money allowing for better response to changing markets, and afford the time for business owners to concentrate solely on running the business.

Local real estate companies rent, lease, or sell commercial space and/or assist in identifying the right business location. Look in the Yellow Pages of local telephone and business directories for a list of private real estate firms.

The Small Business Development Center (Sbdc) Business Incubator

Small starting businesses may opt to locate at the SBDC Business Incubator (the Incubator). The Incubator was first established in 1989 to provide local entrepreneurs with access to affordable space where businesses could be nurtured and helped to survive the start-up period when they are most vulnerable. The Incubator provides:

1) flexible office leases at affordable rates;
2) on-site management, marketing and financial consulting;
3) administrative support services;
4) access to a conference and training room;
5) access to office equipment such as a fax machine, typewriter, computers, printer and the Internet;
6) access to a photocopier; and
7) assistance in obtaining financing necessary for company growth.

To be eligible for tenancy, a business must meet the following criteria: 1) business must be majority-owned by indigenous person(s) as defined by the CNMI Constitution, a U.S. citizen, IR or green card holder; 2) applicant must be a resident of the CNMI; 3) business must demonstrate need for the Incubator and the SBDC's services; 4) requested services must be available; 5) willingness to prepare and work with a realistic business plan; 6) willingness to work with SBDC staff; 7) willingness to share information for proper technical assistance.

For information on space availability, rental rates, and other service offerings, contact:

Small Business Development Center
Northern Marianas College
P.O. Box 501250 C.K.
As Terlaje Campus, Building T
As Terlaje, Saipan, MP 96950
Tel.: (670) 235-1551/1552
Fax: (670) 235-5383

Environmental Impact of Doing Business

The physical structure of your building and the activities you conduct there may possibly have an effect on the environment. The CNMI works hard to protect its environment and preserve its resources for the safety and health of residents and future enjoyment of surroundings and resources. This section highlights the different agencies charged with protecting and preserving the CNMI's land, air, water, coastal resources, fish and wildlife resources and historic and archaeological resources, as well as your obligations while conducting business.

Environmental Quality

Given its mandate to protect the environment and public health, the Division of Environmental Quality (DEQ) develops, implements, and maintains programs that eliminate or minimize threats to the CNMI's land, air and water. Here is a listing of permits issued by DEQ and the forms necessary to complete to obtain each of the different permits.

Division of Environmental Quality Permit Requirements	
Permit	Required Forms/documents
Ownership/Operation of Auto/Heavy Equipment Shops	Plans for paint booths, chemical storage, and used oil management
Use of Pesticides for Structural Treatment	*Pesticide Use for Structural Treatment Permit Application*
Importation of Pesticides	*Notice of Intent to Import Pesticides*
Sale of Pesticides	*Pesticide Dealer's License Application*
Drilling/Installation of Wells	*Well Drilling Permit Application*
Operation of Wells/Withdrawal of Groundwater	*Application for Well Operations Permit; Renewal Well Operations Application*
Licensing of Well Driller	*Well Driller's License Application*
Ownership/Operation of Reverse Osmosis (RO) Units	*Letter of Intent; RO Unit Waste Product IWDS Permit Application; Land Disposal of RO Discharge Permit Application*
Use/Operation of Underground Storage Tanks (UST)	*ST Permit to Operate Application Form; Renewal UST Permit to Operate Application*
Installation of Underground or Above Ground Storage Tanks (AST)	*UST and AST Installation Permit Discharge from Oil/Water Separator, RO & Brinewater Discharge & Application Form; Land Disposal of other Wastewater Permit Application*
Installation of Septic System, Sewage Holding Tanks, Other Wastewater Treatment Systems (OWTS), Temporary Toilet Facility (TTF), Individual Wastewater Disposal System (IWDS)	*IWDS Permit Application*

Source: Division of Environmental Quality

Division of Environmental Quality Permit Requirements	
Pesticide Use Permit for Structural Treatment	$50
Notice of Intent to Import Pesticides -	$0
Pesticide Dealer's License -	$0
Well Drilling Permit	
Test and Monitoring	$100
NEW; based on Discharge Capacity	
< 20 gallons per month (gpm)	$50
21 gpm to 100 gpm	$200
101 gpm to 200 gpm	$1000
201 gpm to 350 gpm	$2000
351 gpm to 500 gpm	$4000
> 500 gpm	$8000
Renewal -	$0
Well Operations Permit	
New (Based on Discharge Capacity)	
< 20 gallons per month (gpm)	$25
21 gpm to 100 gpm	$100
101 gpm to 200 gpm	$500
201 gpm to 350 gpm	$1,000
351 gpm to 500 gpm	$2,000
> 500 gpm	$4,000
Renewal	50% of above fees
Well Driller's License	
New	$10,000
Renewal	$1,000
Underground Storage Tank Permit	
Installation	$500
Operation (New and Renewal)	$150
Individual Wastewater Disposal System Permit	
Multi-Residential	$200
Non-Residential Commercial	$200
Revision	$25
On-site Water Treatment System Permit	$.10/gal plant capacity
Renewal	$25
Septic System and Wastewater Pumpers	
Registration	$200
Earth Moving and Erosion Control Permit (Commercial)	
Up to 1 hectare	$100
> 1 hectare& ≤ 5 hectares	$400
> 5 hectares & ≤ 15 hectares	$800
> 15 hectares & ≤ 50 hectares	$2,000
> 50 hectares & ≤ 100 hectares	$5,000
> 100 hectares & ≤ 200 hectares	$10,000
> 200 hectares	$15,000
401 Water Quality Certification (Commercial)	
> 5000 gals of wastewater/day; clearing of > 1000 sq mtrs; or filling > 1000 cubic mtrs in CNMI waters	$5,000
< 5000 gals of wastewater/day; clearing of < 1000 sq mtrs; or filling < 1000 cubic mtrs in CNMI waters	$1,000

For specific information on human health and environment regulations or permits, contact:

Division of Environmental Quality
P.O. Box 501304
Gualo Rai Commercial Center
Gualo Rai, Saipan, MP 96950
Tel.: (670) 664-8500-Saipan; 532-3102-Rota; 433-3169-Tinian
Fax: (670) 664-8540-Saipan; 532-3103-Rota; 433-3169-Tinian

Coastal Resources

The Coastal Resources Management Office (CRMO) works to protect, conserve and manage the CNMI's coastal resources. Jurisdictions and Areas of Particular Concern (APCs) CRMO has jurisdiction over the Commonwealth Territorial Sea which encompasses the area extending twelve (12) miles beyond the CNMI's archipelagic baseline and all inland areas. This jurisdiction excludes U.S. Government land.

A proposed project wholly or partially within an APC, or which constitutes a Major Siting, or which has a direct and significant impact on an APC requires a CRM permit. There are five (5) APCs:

1.Shoreline	**the area between the mean high water mark or the edge of a shorelinecliff and one hundred fifty (150) feet inland**
2.Lagoon and Reef	**the area extending seaward from the water line to the outer slope of the reef**
3.Wetlands and Mangrove	**those areas which are permanently or periodically covered with water and within which can be found species of wetland or mangrove vegetation**
4.Port and Industrial	**those land and water areas surrounding the commercial ports of Saipan, Tinian and Rota**
5.Coastal Hazards	**the areas identified as coastal flood hazard zones by the Federal Emergency Management Agency (FEMA)**

Major Sitings

A "major siting" refers to any proposed project which has the potential to directly and significantly impact coastal resources within the CNMI. Major Siting projects could also be located within an APC. Such projects vary in scope and size and can include proposed projects with potential for significant adverse effects on submerged lands, groundwater recharge areas, cultural areas, historic or archaeological sites and properties, designated conservation and pristine areas, or uninhabited islands, sparsely populated islands, mangroves, reefs, wetlands, beaches and lakes, areas of significant interest, recreational areas, limestone, volcanic and cocos forest, and endangered or threatened species or marine mammal habitats.

Minor Permits

A Minor Permit is required for projects that are not identified as Major Sitings and are located within an APC. Such projects include the construction of picnic shelters, landscaping and other beautification activities and strip clearing for surveying and construction.

Types of Applications

CRMO has the following types of applications:

1. General Permit Application (for a Major Siting project or any other project located in an APC)
2. Shoreline Permit Application (for general activities within Shoreline APC)
3. Shoreline Permit Application for Photographic Activities
4. Lagoon & Reef Permit Application for Marine Sport Activities
5. Port & Industrial Permit Application for Drydock Activities
6. Shoreline and/or Lagoon & Reef Permit Application for Scientific Research

A pre-application meeting with CRMO and/or CRM Regulatory Agencies or review of plans will determine if a CRM permit is required and if so, what type of permit is required for the proposed project.

The Permit Process

Applicants must file an original and eight (8) copies of the application along with applicable exhibits and attachments. For Major Siting projects, the following are required:

1. Copies of construction plans including CNMI certified engineering and architect designs and floor plans;
2. Plans for excavation, earthmoving and stormwater control;
3. A map showing the distance of all proposed structures from mean high water and wetlands, as shown on APC maps, if applicable;
4. Estimated costs for all improvements affixed to the property;
5. Copies of CNMI and Federal permits including business license, submerged lands lease, and other necessary permits;

6. Names of adjacent property owners and copies of letters sent to them notifying them of the proposed project;
7. Adjacent property description;
8. Estimates of daily peak demand for utilities including water and electricity and projected usage of utilities and other infrastructure;
9. Map of the vicinity
10. Topographic survey map with ten (10) foot contour;
11. Elevation plans of the project including a side profile of the project;
12. Title documents to all real property and submerged lands including leases from appropriate parties;
13. Affidavit or declaration made under penalty of perjury that the application is a statement of truth by the principal or authorized agent;
14. Environmental Assessments to include:

a. Project summary, justification and size;

b. Description of existing environment of site including vegetation, wildlife, land uses, historic and cultural resources, soil, geology, topography, weather, and air quality;

c. Description of socio-economic characteristics of the project including income and employment, education, infrastructures, law enforcement, fire protection, hospital, and medical facilities;

d. Discussion of alternatives to the proposed project size/design and how the preferred alternative was selected;

e. Description of the direct, indirect, and cumulative environmental and socio-economic effects, both positive and negative, which may result from the project i.e. air and water quality, noise and dust levels, sedimentation and erosion, plant and wildlife habitat and populations, infrastructure capacity (short and long term);

f. Description of how impacts have been avoided or minimized and how any unavoidable impacts will be mitigated.

A non-refundable application fee is assessed on all applications.

Coastal Resources Management Office Permit Fee Schedule	
Permit Type	Fee
Government Project Permit -	$0
Emergency Permit	$25
Minor Permit	$100
Marine Sports	$100
Jet Ski Operation	
New	$500
Renewal	$400
Other	
Project Cost is less than or equal to $50,000	$100
Project Cost is $50,001 to $100,000	$200
Project Cost is $100,001 to $500,000	$750
Project Cost is $500,001 to $1,000,000	$1,500
Project Cost exceeds $1,000,000 *	

Source: Office of Coastal Resources Management

Note: * $1,500 plus an additional amount equal to the fee for the cost increment exceeding $1,000,000. For example, a project that costs $1,350,000 would be assessed a fee of $2,250 (a $1,500 fee for the first $1,000,000 and a $750 fee for the $350,000 cost increment exceeding $1,000,000). A project that costs $2,000,001 would be assessed a fee of $3,100 ($1,500 for the first $1,000,000, $1,500 for the second $1,000,000 and $100 for the $1.00 increment over $2,000,000). The maximum total fee for any project shall be $300,000.

Major Siting permit applications are reviewed by CRMO and CRM Regulatory Agencies:

1. Department of Lands and Natural Resources (DLNR)
2. Department of Public Works (DPW)
3. Department of Commerce (DOC)
4. Division of Environmental Quality (DEQ)
5. Historic Preservation Office (HPO)
6. Commonwealth Utilities Corporation (CUC)

Among the criteria used in evaluating permit applications are:

Are practical and reasonable alternatives available?
Does the proposed project fit with nearby land and shoreline areas?
Does the project meet Federal and CNMI air and water quality standards?

Upon receipt of a complete application, CRMO and CRM Program Agencies have up to sixty (60) days to issue a final decision on Major Siting applications.

Some Minor Permits require a decision within ten (10) working days by CRMO while other Minor Permits require a decision within sixty (60) days by CRMO and CRM Regulatory Agencies.

Major Sitings require a public hearing. Written comments on projects may be submitted to CRMO to be made part of the permit record and considered in the permit decision.

For more information on coastal permits, contact:

Coastal Resources Management Office
Office of the Governor
Caller Box 10007
2nd Floor, Morgen Building
San Jose, Saipan, MP 96950
Tel.: (670) 664-8300/8301-Saipan; 532-0464-Rota; 433-0494-Tinian
Fax: (670) 664-8315-Saipan; 532-1000-Rota; 433-0638-Tinian
Website: www.crm.gov.mp

Projects near coastal waters or wetlands may also require permits from the U.S. Army Corps of Engineers. For information on whether special permits are required for specific projects, contact:

Department of the Army
Pacific Ocean Division
Corps of Engineers
Guam Operations Office
Room 302 San Ramon Building
115 San Ramon Street
Agana, Guam 96910
Tel.: (671) 472-8091

Fish And Wildlife Resources

Proposed developments that involve hunting, catching or gathering of fish and wildlife or other activities that may impact these resources should consult with the Department of Lands and Natural Resources' Division of Fish and Wildlife to determine if any permits are required for such activities.

The Division of Fish and Wildlife has three (3) Wildlife Conservation/Critical Habitat Areas: 1) Bird Island Wildlife Conservation Area, 2) Kagman Wildlife Conservation Area, and 3) Marpi Commonwealth Forest.

The islands of Guguan, Farallon de Parjaros, Asuncion and Maug are Wildlife Sanctuaries making it illegal to take wildlife species from these islands. Except for cases of emergency, landing on these islands must first be approved by the Director of Fish and Wildlife.

Persons interested in obtaining fish and wildlife permits must fill out a Fishing, Harvesting and Hunting Permit Application and pay the applicable fees. This table lists the types of permits available, their fees and period of validity.

Fish and Wildlife Permits, Fees and Period of Validity

Permit Type	Fee	Period of Validity
Scientific Research	$10	Year
Import/Export	$10	Year
Trochus		
Harvester	$10	Season
Buyer	$5,000	Season
Net(s)		
Commercial	$25	Year
Non-Commercial		
Resident	$5	Year
Non-Resident	$20	Year
Coral	$15	Year
Sea Cucumber		
Harvester - Commercial	$10	Season
Buyer	$25	Season
Aquarium		
Collecting		
Personal	$10	Year
Commercial	$30	Year
Displaying	$30	Year
Hunting		
CNMI Resident		
Each Species	$5	Season
All Species	$20	Season
Non-Resident		
Each Species	$20	Season
All Species	$100	Season

Source: Division of Fish and Wildlife

For more information on fish and wildlife resources and permits, contact:

Division of Fish and Wildlife
Department of Lands and Natural Resources
P.O. Box 10007
Lower Base, Saipan, MP 96950
Tel.: (670) 664-6000-Saipan; 532-6000-Rota; 433-9298-Tinian
Fax: (670) 664-6060-Saipan; 532-0520-Rota; 433-3152-Tinian

HISTORIC AND ARCHAEOLOGICAL RESOURCES

Public Law 3-39, the Historic Preservation Act of 1982, created the Division of Historic Preservation under the Department of Community and Cultural Affairs to ensure the protection of historic, archaeological, architectural and cultural resources. To fulfill its duties, the Division of Historic Preservation reviews public and private land use activities.

The Division of Historic Preservation works closely with the Division of Environmental Quality and the Coastal Resources Management Office. Permits are not issued by these offices if the Division of Historic Preservation finds that the use of subject lands will adversely affect valuable historic property. The types of activities requiring historic preservation review include:

1)Projects requiring Earthmoving Permits - projects requiring mechanized vegetation clearing and earthmoving activities including removing vegetation with a backhoe, payloader or bulldozer, sand or soil mining;

2)Projects requiring Coastal Resource Management (CRM) Permits - projects that are large-scale or with activities within the shoreline, lagoons, reefs, wetlands, mangroves, port/industrial areas, coastal flood zones, and other sensitive environmental areas;

3)Projects which receive federal funding or require federal permits;

4)Projects which will affect historic structures or buildings.

For assistance in filling out the Application for Historic Preservation Review or for further information on the historic preservation review process, contact:

Division of Historic Preservation
Department of Community and Cultural Affairs
Saipan, MP 96950
Tel.: (670) 664-2120-Saipan; 532-0818-Rota; 433-0220-Tinian
Fax: (670) 664-2139-Saipan; 532-0818-Rota; 433-0220-Tinian

Physical Location
Applications and Instructions Mentioned in This section That You May Need

Tip: Print this list, ☑ check all that apply and carry with you

☐ Applications for Building Permit/Plan Review/Floodplain
☐ Pesticide Use for Structural Treatment Permit Application
☐ Notice of Intent to Import Pesticides
☐ Pesticide Dealer's License Application
☐ Well Drilling Permit Application
☐ Application for Well Operations Permit
☐ Renewal Well Operations Application
☐ Well Driller's License Application
☐ Letter of Intent
☐ RO Unit Waste Product IWDS Permit Application
☐ Land Disposal of RO Discharge Permit Application
☐ UST Permit to Operate Application Form
☐ Renewal UST Permit to Operate Application
☐ UST and AST Installation Permit Application Form
☐ Land Disposal of Oil/Water Separator Discharge, RO and Brinewater Discharge and other Wastewater Permit Application
☐ IWDS Permit Application
☐ Septic System and Wastewater Pumpers Registration
☐ Earthmoving and Erosion Control Commercial Permit
☐ 401 Water Quality Certification
☐ General Permit Application
☐ Shoreline Permit Application
☐ Shoreline Permit Application for Photographic Activities
☐ Lagoon & Reef Permit Application for Marine Sport Activities
☐ Port & Industrial Permit Application for Drydock Activities
☐ Shoreline and/or Lagoon & Reef Permit Application for Scientific Research

- ☐ Fishing, Harvesting and Hunting Permit Application
- ☐ Application for Historic Preservation Review
- ☐ Application for Utility Service
- ☐ CUC Dedication of Easement
- ☐ Site Location Sketch

Utility Service

For more information on utility services, contact:

Commonwealth Utilities Corporation
P.O. Box 501220
Joeten Commercial Building
Dandan, Saipan, MP 96950
Tel.: (670) 235-7025-Saipan; 532-4010-Rota; 433-9264-Tinian
Fax: (670) 235-6145-Saipan; 532-9415-Rota; 433-9262-Tinian

Phone Service

IT&E is the one provider of land lines on Saipan.

IT&E formerly Pacific Telecom, Inc. may be contacted at
P.O. Box 500437
Chalan Laulau, Saipan, MP 96950
Tel: (670) 234-7143; Fax: (670) 682-4555
Rota: (670) 532-3599; fax: (670) 532-0101
Tinian: (670) 433-0210; fax: (670) 433-0211
Website: www.pticom.com

Hiring Employees

At present, the Dept of Labor and Immigration is going through transition.

1. Division of Labor, and the
2. Division of Employment Services, both c/o

CNMI Department of Labor
Caller Box 10007
2nd Floor, Afetna Square Building
San Antonio, Saipan, MP 96950
Tel.: (670) 236-0900/0907-Saipan; 532-9429-Rota; 433-3700-Tinian
Fax: (670) 236-0991-Saipan; 532-9468-Rota; 433-3730-Tinian

Guest Worker Program

The following Guest Worker/ Transitional Worker/ Non-Immigrant Worker / Contract Worker Hiring Process applies to the 5-year period of time from November 28, 2009 to November 2014. At the end of that period, the reliance on and possibility of hiring guest workers will end. At that time, only people with valid US citizen/resident/immigrant status may be hired for employment.

Anyone doing business on Saipan during this period may use the following checklist to negotiate the process of hiring employees.

☐ Post Job Vacancy Announcement. First, it is expected that every effort will be made by employers to hire US citizens for positions of employment. List the job vacancy with the Department of Employment Services.

☐ During the Umbrella Period (Nov 28, 2009 - Nov 28, 2011) a guest with an "Umbrella" permit may be hired for employment. The period of that employment may not extend past the end of the Transitional period which ends Nov 2014.

[] During the Transitional Period if a non-resident worker is required to be hired, the employer must sponsor this individual.
Complete form I-129CW Petition for a Non-Immigrant Worker in the CNMI
$320 application fee
$ 80 biometric fee
$150 Education funding fee
CW-1 status lasts for one year

Chapter 7
Interview with a Saipan Business Success Story

Tony Pellegrino has a long and storied history on Saipan. He is a serial entrepreneur, mentor, philanthropist, writer, husband and father. Tony has lived on Saipan since 1980. His current businesses include Saipan Ice and Water (1985), the first bottled water company on Saipan; Sunset Cruises, the longest-running tourism company on the island (1984); Syaquaculture, Saipan's first shrimp farm (2005), among others.

He's has launched successful businesses, and let go of other less successful ones walking away from millions along the way, but always keeping on the plus side of success.

His generosity has resulted in the establishment of a library, many apartment complexes, schools and churches on the island. He recently launched the Northern Marianas Trades Institute (2008) with the mission of training Saipan residents in viable trades such as plumbing, painting, electrical repair and construction.

Born in America, he has lived in Italy, Japan, Hawaii and the US mainland. Tony also writes a weekly column for the Saipan Tribune. No book about doing business on Saipan would be complete without the valuable insights of this dynamic, creative, and successful individual.

Walt: What sort of advice would you give to me if I were seeking to launch a business in the CNMI?

Tony: If I were sitting and giving advice to you, the first thing I would want to know is what sort of background you are bringing to Saipan. Were you an employee all your life, or were you an employer? If you've been an employee, you're going to have to develop new ways of thinking and acting. Being an employee doesn't prepare you for what it takes to be a successful entrepreneur.

If, on the other hand, you've been an employer, business owner in the past, then you should already have the right attitude towards risk, opportunity, marketing and business in general.

Tony: So, say you have an idea of a new business to start. I would then want to give you some advice on what island to concentrate on.

Saipan is a small island. There are about 35,000 people on island, plus 13,000 non-resident workers--that number is decreasing. The two neighboring islands have no more than about 3,000 people combined. Logistically, it's difficult and expensive to ship between the islands. For example, for my water company, I don't have a location on either Tinian or Rota. I don't ship my water over there. 94% of the population is on Saipan. 94% of the economic activity is here. So, forget about the other two islands unless you have an internet based business that isn't limited by the geography.

The next step is, decide who is going to be your market? Are you dealing with local people, creating something on Saipan and exporting, or do you want to import or will it be a domestic business catering to tourists?

Walt: What do you think about starting a franchise here on Saipan?

Tony: Beware of franchises; Do your market research. How much is the building going to cost, initial supplies, royalties, equipment. It can get very expensive, and most importantly, there's simply not enough traffic here to support it. People here on Saipan aren't going to drive 2 miles to get a pretzel. Pizza? Same thing. Where is the traffic? Franchises like Scoops and Big Dipper [ice cream franchises] just couldn't survive here on Saipan. Starbucks? Can you get 100 people a day to buy coffee? I'm not too sure.

Walt: Is that why Wendy's failed here on Saipan?

Tony: I think so. Not enough traffic. McDonald's on the other hand, continues to be successful for a number of reasons. One, he was the first. Two, McDonald's has a stronger brand identity, and the trademark arches make it a much more visible symbol in the community.

Walt: What are the best industries to get into?
Tony: To me, there's two major industries that will save this economy.

The first is tourism. If we can learn to do a better job, we could double our numbers. It's not about money, it's ideas. For one thing we need to get more of the population involved in making our guests feel welcomed. These days, it's only the businesses that care about the tourists...the local population doesn't. But, they should participate. Most local people don't greet the tourists...Tourism is everybody's job.

The second is agriculture. It's a sleeping giant. With the land in Tinian, Rota and Saipan, we could feed all the military on Guam, export to Korea and Japan and more. Japan is only three hours away by plane; one or two days by boat. We could and should be export ing so many fruits and vegetables. We're supplying nothing to the troops in Guam right now. I hope to change that. Not many people realize this, but after WWII, Saipan fed all the military troops in Guam and Saipan. There were 200,000 troops we were feeding. Think about that!

There are lot of farmers, but they're all separated—doing their own thing. They grow the crops, but they don't have the outlet. There needs to be one guy who has the market; one guy who is the intermediary to the overseas markets.

Walt: What other ideas for businesses have you thought about?
Tony: When I lived in Hawaii, I would always go to different restaurants and bakeries. When you go to a Chinese restaurant in Hawaii, you can get these great Chinese cookies. There's a bakery counter at the front, so right after every meal, as you're leaving, you can take home some of these pastries. There's not a good pastry or pie making company on Saipan. I've never seen a Chinese bakery shop specializing in Chinese pastries. People like sweets. You could sell to the restaurants rather than open up your own shop.

I also think some uniquely Saipan handicrafts, wood carvings, story boards, like they have from Palau. We need to create something similar that's identified with Saipan and Saipan only.

Debt Management. I've noticed over the years, for whatever reason, there's a lack of sophistication in business and personal financing. People start great business ideas, but then end up mismanaging it into the ground. 95% of the failure of a business is mismanagement. There needs to be some sort of certified money management course or trainer, some sort of business mentorship, incubator for local businesses.

Tony: Some of the best business ideas are not about doing something new. In other words, you don't have to come up with something radical. You can do something that someone else is doing, but simply run it a little smarter. You know, I don't have better tasting water. If I gave you three glasses of water, one from my company and two from my competitors, you wouldn't be able to tell the difference. The way I set myself apart is by offering better customer service. I impress that on my employees. It's the little things like how you greet the customer, how you interact with them that sets you apart.

It's because of customer service. I'm a firm believer in building a winning relationship with customers. Smile. Offer unexpected value. Make the customer happy. Even if you take a loss at times, it's always better to have a customer walk away satisfied. *It doesn't always have to be new, but it should always be better!*

Walt: Don't you think some kinds of products and services are just too mainstream, to American to be adopted here given the lifestyle and habits?
Tony: Well, with any new idea, there's going to be learning curve. It may take people a while to adapt to something new, but if you stick with it, and if it's a good idea, it can work. Back in 1985, when I set up my first water plant, I tried to get people to get buy bottle water. Before that, people were using their rain catchment tanks and dealing with bird droppings, ants, leaves in their water. We offered Reverse Osmosis, filtration, things people weren't familiar with.

"Why should I buy from you?" they would ask. I took it to the stores. Some stores didn't want to carry it. So, I gave them on consignment. I did television advertising. It took me 3 years to get people to start buying bottled water. I was the first. Now they love it. Now I have 12 competitors...There's not much alien to the population anymore...ipod, cell phone, people are very familiar with the latest technology, so the acceptability curve today is very short.

It also depends on who you sell to. There are essentially 3 classes of people here on Saipan.
5,000 people in government x 3 people per household = 15,000
18,000 non-resident = 13,000
and the have nots*: 7,000 households x 3 per household = 21,000

Those people in government, with steady incomes and fancy cars can afford the items that you think might be too mainstream. They are the ones who go to the restaurants, buy the cars, donate to charities, etc.

**According to Tony, there are about 7,000 households on welfare.*

Walt: Do you have partners in your businesses:
Tony: Never.

Walt: People say that the higher minimum wage will make it difficult for businesses on Saipan to survive. What do you say about that?
Tony: When the minimum wage is so low, you can afford more workers and people get inefficient. However, if we incorporate the latest ways of doing business, we don't need as many workers. At my plant, we use modern equipment, so we use 2 guys instead of 6 to do the same amount of work.

Recently, I had to let go 15 out of 60 workers. Those who were left, we showed them how to work more efficiently. We showed them how to improve operations with less people. Everywhere else in the country has to operate with a

$7.25/hour minimum wage. We can't keep paying people $3.50/hour forever. We have to become more competitive, streamline our businesses and compete with the rest of the world.

Walt: What's your take on Federalization?
Tony: A lot of people are against federalization. I feel that it's going to allow the local people to take back their island, and that's especially important given that non-residents outnumber the locals. As a result of relying too much on contract workers, we've lost our work ethic. We are going to relearn certain skills, regenerate our work ethic, get back all the things we lost. Federalization will make this easier.

Walt: What do you mean? What's been lost?

There are 70 beauty shops all run by non-resident workers. There are over 120 auto mechanics, over 120, 10% or less are owned by local people. Almost all the skilled trades people are contract workers. There are 140 grocery stores, 95% owned by Chinese and Koreans. 99cent is Korean owned. Payless is Korean-owned. Now, I'm not against business owners from other countries coming here and becoming successful. I'd simply like to see more ownership in the hands of the local population.

Before we opened the doors to the migrant worker, who were the plumbers and tradespeople? Who did all the work? It was the local people. It made us dependent. I'm 125% in favor of federalization

There's a whole new economic picture evolving. People, especially the local community need to prepare now, because by 2014 [when all the contract workers are phased out] it's over.

Tony: Let me ask you a question. What is Saipan's number one export right now? We are exporting money. It's true. We import labor, but we export money. A lot of our contract workers send money back to their countries.

We need to bring in money. Import money. Until we import money, we will not become prosperous. Culture is great, but can you take it to the bank? Can you eat it? Can you feed your kids with it?

The way to import money is to export something of value. That's what we need to do. It's the only way to prosper.

Walt: What about corruption? Has any of the government corruption we always hear about presented any roadblocks to your business?
Tony: I think years ago, that might have been true. I don't think that happens very often now. But, you're always going to run into some opposition with any new idea—not necessarily from corrupt officials, but from just about anybody who gets jealous or who wants to block you for whatever reason.

But what I see as a road block to progress is simply the size of government. Why do we have over 4,000 people in the government? 10 people per legislator. There are just too many people in government, and too much political patronage. That's our biggest obstacle on Saipan. If we get rid of that, we'll see a great improvement in life, the economy, the work ethic, and doing business on Saipan.

Extra! Tony's Advice for Foreign Entrepreneurs

As this book was nearing completion, someone asked me what sort of advice I would give to a foreign business owner seeking to do business on Saipan. So, I asked Tony for his insights.

Walt: You started a car wash franchise and coin-operated lockers in Japan. You started the first office cleaning franchise in Japan. What advice would you give to entrepreneurs coming from Japan or any foreign country?
Tony: 1. Get to know the lay of the land first. When I was living in Japan, I came here three times on my own for research before I came for good. I fell in love with life on Saipan. "Is this for real?" I asked myself. "Do I really want to move to Saipan?" "What's it really like to live and do business here?"

I came once with a guide, and two times on my own. I walked the streets. I hung out in the bars. I talked to people. I didn't come in as the stereotypical loud American. Unless you're a Forbes 100 CEO, don't swagger in thinking you know everything. Learn the local customs. Take your time. Assimilate.

2. Find a reputable partner or agent. This is very important. There are people here who've been around for a while. Wheelers and dealers who have reputations that everyone knows. Hooking up with the wrong person will affect YOUR reputation and could be the kiss of death for your business. Everyone says they should be the one to open doors for you. Do your due diligence to find the right person.

3. Don't give control away. The goal of finding a local rep or agent is to help you get acclimated, not to run your business for you. The strength of your business is based on the personal relationships you form with people, so don't give control away to anyone else.

Chapter 8:

I'm Ready! What should I do next?

Now that you're ready to move forward, here is my suggested list of things to think about, do and accomplish in order to start doing business on Saipan.

SUMMARY

☐ Research the island

☐ Find the lines of communication

☐ Find an agent or on-island contact

☐ Visit the island as often as necessary

☐ Take the "Doing Business on Saipan" Tour

☐ Make yourself known

☐ Observe the culture/Ask questions

☐ Find out what is needed or wanted on Saipan

☐ Resolve to deliver what is needed or wanted

☐ Use the Master Checklist

SUMMARY DETAILS

☐ Research the island

Read books, visit websites, watch videos

☐ Find the lines of communication

Make a comprehensive list of the people, clients, customers, government officials, friends, investors, suppliers and supporters who need to know about your new business venture, or with whom you will need to communicate as your launch and grow your business.

☐ Find an agent or on-island contact

Heed Tony Pellegrino's advice for foreign investors and carefully choose and appoint someone on island to submit documents, make arrangements on your behalf. You may, of course, accomplish this on your own via mail, fax, email, wire transfer and telephone.

☐ Visit the island as often as necessary

Photographs, videos, email cannot replace the information you gather by actually being on Saipan. Come see for yourself.

☐ Take the "Doing Business on Saipan" Tour

Once you're here, consider taking our tour to familiarize you with the island, the business districts, important offices and associations.

☐ Observe the culture/Ask questions

Don't make the mistake of assuming that life and business on Saipan is the same as that of your home country. Take the time to spend weeks and even months simply making acquaintances, observing the flow of life and asking questions

☐ Make yourself known

As you move forward, begin to inform the people and organizations on your "Communication Lines" list of your arrival and intentions. Of course, a certain amount of secrecy is always advisable to maintain your competitive advantage.

☐ Find out what is needed or wanted on Saipan

What does the island require? What do the people want? What do the government agencies require of you in order to legally do business on Saipan?

☐ Resolve to deliver what is needed or wanted

Once you fully understand what is needed or wanted, then simply make a conscious decision to compile, create, develop, produce, market and deliver what is needed or wanted.

☐ Use the Master Checklist to help you deliver what is needed or wanted

Your ABSOLUTE FIRST STEP:

Assuming you know what kind of business you want to launch, and assuming you know which part of the island you wish to set up your business, the very first thing you should do is call or visit the Zoning office in Dan Dan to find out if the location you are considering is "zoned" for the specific type of activity you are considering. Once your zoning application is approved, you can move forward with the other requirements (permits, licenses, etc.)….

☑ The Master Checklist for Starting a Business on Saipan

Assuming you have a business plan and marketing strategy....

Do Immediately

☐ Contact Zoning Office, Business license office; view their websites

☐ Contact all relevant offices (see Business Offices Chart in appendix) and make yourself known

☐ Compile list of all forms you will need and download or request from the appropriate offices

☐ Review all forms thoroughly to determine if there are any unforeseen, unanticipated barriers (pay close attention to insurance requirements, immigration/entry requirements, environmental, etc.)

☐ If there are any special circumstances that may affect your applications or approval (police record, citizenship status, etc.), please call the appropriate office NOW to start the communication process.

☐ Secure any necessary visas/entry permits if possible

Have Ready

☐ Collect, copy and compile passports, photos, birth certificates, etc.

☐ Collect, copy and compile any and all documentation that supports your legitimacy, solvency and good faith, whether needed or not

Do to Register Your Business

☐ Decide on your business structure, name, logo, etc.

☐ Reserve your website domain name; start developing website

☐ Order *Saipan Atlas(.saipanliving.com),* download Zoning Maps

☐ Obtain listings of office space, land for lease, businesses for sale

☐ With the help of your agent, choose several possible locations

☐ Confirm that your locations are zoned for your type of business

☐ Inquire about insurance requirements and get quotes

☐ Complete the Zoning Inquiry Form

☑ *The Master Checklist (page 2),*

☐ File Incorporation or Partnership documents as necessary ($)

☐ Get Zoning approval

☐ Apply for Business License; pay fee ($)

For Sole proprietorships

☐ Get Zoning approval

☐ Apply for Business License

☐ Pay Business License Fee

☐ Complete Business License Application (receive same day)

For Corporations

☐ Download latest checklist[2] (Visit http://www.commerce.gov.mp)

☐ Get zoning approval (The Zoning office is across hall from Business License office)

☐ Apply for business license[2] (office is located in Dan Dan on the 2nd flr of Joeten Bld)

☐ Create and notarize your own Articles of Incorporation.
(Only one officer of corporation need sign articles; a template you can use for your own Articles of Incorporation is available saipanliving.com/business/articles.pdf)

☐ Create and notarize your own Agent Consent Form
(Only one officer of corporation needs to sign articles)

☐ Create your own Corporation's Bylaws
(These need not be notarized; They may also be filed at a later date. We recommend doing everything at once. A template you can use for your own Articles of Incorporation is available at www.saipanliving.com/business/articles.pdf)

☐ File Articles of Incorporation, Agent Consent Form, & By Laws with Registrar of Corporations (Submit in triplicate; one original plus two copies; The Registrar of Corporations is located on Capital Hill in the _______ Building)

☐ Pay total filing fee of $125; ($100 for articles of incorporation; $25 for bylaws)
After your corporate filing is processed, you will be issued a Certificate of Authority within a few weeks. With this, you can open your bank account. You may use the receipt from the filing to complete your business license application process.

☐ Complete the business license application form and pay appropriate fee.

☐ File initial Corporate Report & pay $50 fee
(This must be done within 60 days of the date of your initial corporate filing)

☐ NOTE: Other filings for which you may be responsible include

- BGRT (Quarterly Business Gross Revenue Tax)
- Corporate Report (January 1, and March 1 of every year)
- Annual renewal of your business license; All tax returns must be filed and you must be in good standing in order to renew your business license.

☑ *The Master Checklist (page 3),*

According to Pam Halstead of the Business License Office, "The business license is just the first step! If all your papers are in order, I can grant you a business license the same day you apply. But that's just the beginning. Depending on your business category, there may be other requirements you need to fulfill."

Do after Business License is approved

☐ Finalize lease/rent agreement

Please note the following if these scenarios apply to you

☐ I am offering a new service in an existing office space
- make sure location has not been rezoned
- apply for new certificate of occupancy

☐ I am occupying or starting a new food service establishment
- certificate of occupancy
- Board of Health approval

☐ I am offering a tourist-related service/tour, marine/boat/jet ski ride
- Secure Insurance compliance
- Coastal Resources Management approval

☐ Apply for any required special licenses, permits or certificates ($)
- ☐ Food Handlers Permit ($)
- ☐ Alcohol/Tobacco License ($)
- ☐ Sanitary Permit ($)
- ☐ Certificate of Occupancy ($)

Do while securing necessary permits and approvals

☐ Open a bank account

☐ Set up utilities

☐ Set up phone service, internet access for your business space

☑ *The Master Checklist (page4),*

Do to secure employees as necessary

NOTE: Labor/Immigration regulations are in a state of transition right now. Stay tuned to saipanliving.com and destinationsaipan for updates.

☐ Register with workers comp

☐ Secure necessary insurance for employees or business activity

☐ Post job vacancy announcements

Do to launch Marketing & PR strategy

☐ Launch website

☐ Execute "Websites that Sell" Checklist*

☐ Launch Marketing strategy to reach customers

**For a thorough checklist steps to maximize your internet presence and online marketing strategy, check out The 24 Hour Quickstart Internet Manual at www.passionprofit.com*

Appendix

Forms
Zoning Inquiry Form
Zoning Application
Corporate Checklist
LLC Checklist
Business license Application (3 pages)
Resources

Zoning Inquiry

COMMONWEALTH
ZONING BOARD

Commonwealth of the Northern Mariana Islands
Zoning Office, Caller Box 10007, Saipan, MP 96950
Tel. 670-234-9661, Fax. 670-234-9666, E-mail: staff@zoning.gov.mp

Record of Zoning Inquiry

File Number	Received By
Date Received	Date Filed

The Zoning Office is pleased to answer your questions. Please fill in the information below.

Contact Name:	
Company:	
Address:	
E-mail:	Phone:
Lot #:	Fax:
Village:	Street:
Describe location of property & building name:	

Describe the type of business: ____

__ I'm buying an existing business and/or structure with no change of use or new construction.
__ I'm renewing a business license or Certificate of Occupancy with no change in the location.
__ I'm renewing a business license and changing the location.
__ I'm starting a new business in a (check one): home __ commercial structure __.
__ I'm relocating a business from ____ to ____
__ I'm adding a new line of business at an existing location
Describe the existing business ____
Describe the new business ____
__ Other ____
Submitted By ____ Date ____

Zoning Office Use
Zoning District: AG __ BR __ GE __ GC __ IN __ MC __ PR __ RU __ TR __ VC __ VR __ ABO __
Use Category (from Table 1) ____
__ Zoning approval is not required for the activity described above because:
____
__ Zoning application is required. __ Permit Application __ Nonconforming Use.
__ The proposed use is not permitted in the zoning district (see Section 404, Table 1, Saipan Zoning Law).
Signature of Zoning Official ____ Date ____
Signature of Zoning Official ____ Date ____

Record of Zoning Inquiry 3-19-09

The full zoning law of 2008 may be downloaded at http://zoning.gov.mp/ where you will also find a complete list of relevant forms and applications.

Zoning Permit Application 1 of 2

COMMONWEALTH
ZONING BOARD

Commonwealth of the Northern Mariana Islands
Zoning Office, Caller Box 10007, Saipan, MP 96950
Tel. 670-234-9661, E-mail: staff@zoning.gov.mp

Zoning Permit Application

File Number	Received By
Date Received	Date Filed

SITE INFORMATION	
1. Development Name:	2. Zoning District:
3. Lot Number(s):	4. Lot area: sq. m.
5. Village:	6. Street Name:
7. Use(s) (from Table 1, SZL)	
APPLICANT INFORMATION (use name order: Given Name, Middle Name, Family Name)	
8. Applicant Name:	
Company:	Phone:
Mailing Address:	Fax:
E-mail:	
9. Contact person (if different):	Phone:
E-mail:	Fax:
Mailing Address:	
10. Lessee (if different):	Phone:
E-mail:	Fax:
Mailing Address:	
11. Property Owner Name (if not applicant):	Phone:
E-mail:	Fax:
Mailing Address:	
12. Applicant is (check all that are appropriate) Property Owner ____ Lessee ____ Developer ____ Other (describe)	
13. Describe the location of the property or provide street address:	

Page 1 of 2

Zoning Permit Application 3-19-09

The full zoning law of 2008 may be downloaded at http://zoning.gov.mp/ where you will also find a complete list of relevant forms and applications.

Zoning Permit Application 2 of 2

14. Describe the current use of property including number of dwelling units and size of structure(s):

15. Describe your proposal:

DECLARATION

I (We) consent to the entry in or upon the premises described in this application by any authorized official of the Office of the Zoning Administrator or Hearing Officer for the purpose of inspection and of posting, maintaining, and removing such notices as may be required by law.

Applicant

I declare under the penalty of perjury that the above statements and answers, and the attached documents, are true and correct.

____________________ Date: __________

Signature

____

Printed Name in English

Lessee or Property Owner

I declare under the penalty of perjury that I am the owner or lessee of the property under consideration in this application and that the above statements and answers, and the attached documents, are true and correct. If I am not the sole owner of the property, I also declare, under the penalty of perjury, that I am acting with the consent of all appropriate owners of the property, including, but not limited to, owners in fee simple, lessees and sublessees, joint tenants, tenants in common and any other legally recognized forms of ownership under CNMI law.

____________________ Date: __________

Signature

Printed Name in English

Required enclosures: Depending on the proposal, additional information may be required.

Page 2 of 2

Zoning Permit Application 3-19-09

The full zoning law of 2008 may be downloaded at http://zoning.gov.mp/ where you will also find a complete list of relevant forms and applications.

Corporate filing Checklist

REGISTRAR OF CORPORATIONS
Department of Commerce

CHECK LIST

Name of Corporation: ______________________

Date Received: ____________ Payment Receipt No.: ____________

ADDRESS:
Completed documents to be sent to: ______________________

Phone Number: ____________ Submitted by: ____________

- -

ARTICLES OF INCORPORATION:

1. ____ a. Original and Two Copies
   b. Fees: Articles of Incorporation $100
   Bylaws $25.00
2. ____ Name of Corporation: must satisfies the requirement of 4 CMC § 4321; must contain the word "corporation", "incorporated", "company", or "limited", or the abbreviations.
3. ____ Number of shares that the corporation is authorized to issue;
4. ____ The address of the corporation's initial registered office;
5. ____ The name of the initial agent at that office;
   (The consent of the Registered Agent must be attached to the Articles of Incorporation)
6. ____ The name and address of each incorporators;
7. ____ The Article of Incorporation must be signed and dated.

The Articles of incorporation MAY set forth:

a. ____ The purpose or purposes for which the corporation is organized
b. ____ Managing the business and regulating the affairs of the corporation;
c. ____ Defining, limiting, and regulating the powers of the corporation, its board of directors, and shareholders;
d. ____ A par value for authorized shares or classes of shares;
e. ____ The imposition of personal liability on shareholders for the debts of the corporation to a specific extent and upon specific conditions; and
f. ____ Any provision that under this part are required or permitted to be set forth in the bylaws;
g. ____ The Articles of incorporation need not set forth any of the corporate powers enumerated in this part.

Corporation Documents Picked up by: ______________________

Date: ______________________

Business License Application 1 of 3

DIVISION OF REVENUE AND TAXATION
DEPARTMENT OF FINANCE

P.O. Box 5234 CHRB SAIPAN, MP 96950 TEL. (670) 664-1000 FAX. (670) 664-1015

APPLICATION FOR BUSINESS LICENSE

A. TYPE OF APPLICATION

☐ New Taxpayer's I.D. No.: ____

☐ Renewal -Business License No. ____ Federal Employee I.D. No.: ____

1st Year of Operation: ____

☐ Amendment (check below)

☐ Additional Location ☐ Additional line(s) of business (please speicfy below) ☐ Change of location

☐ Add D.B.A. ☐ Request for duplicate license(s) ☐ Change of business name

B. APPLICATION INFORMATION

1. Form of business and name of applicant

☐ Sole Proprietorship ____

☐ Partnership ____ (attach partnership papers)

☐ Corporation ____ (attach incorporation papers)

☐ check if foreign corporation

☐ LLC ____ (attach organization documents)

☐ Joint Venture ____ (attach joint venture agreement)

☐ Other ____ (please specify)

(Note: Attachment requested above need not be submitted on renewal application unless there are changes to the original information provided)

2. Mailing address: ____ Tel: ____ Fax: ____

C. LINE(S) OF BUSINESS APPLIED FOR (List every activity location separately)

	Line of Business	DBA (assumed name)	Island	Village	Lot No.
1.					
2.					
3.					
4.					
5.					
6.					
7.					
8.					

If the applicant is a foreign corporation or a NON CNMI resident, please specify the name of the registered resident agent below.

Name ____ Mailing address ____ Tel: ____

D. APPLICANT DECLARATION

I declare under penalty of perjury that the information above are true and correct and that I have complied with all Commonwealth laws and regulations for purposes of obtaining a business license. This Declaration is made on this ____ Day of ____ at ____

Print applicant's name Signature Title Date

Official Use Only

The applicant ☐ is ☐ is not recommended for approval for the issuance of a business license. Reviewed by ____ Date ____

Approved by ____ Date ____ Date license issued ____ Lic. No. ____

License fee paid: $ ____ Penalty: $ ____ Date Paid ____ Receipt No.

Original Business License Office Yellow Workers Compensation Office Pink Applicant

The latest application may be downloaded at http://cnmidof.net/ where you will also find a complete list of relevant forms and applications.

Business License Application 2 of 3

DIVISION OF REVENUE AND TAXATION
DEPARTMENT OF FINANCE

P.O. Box 5234 CHRB SAIPAN, MP 96950 TEL (670) 664-1000 FAX (670) 664-1015

BUSINESS LICENSE APPLICATION **REQUIREMENTS**

	SOLE PROPRIETOR		CORPORATION		PARTNERSHIP		LLC		NON-PROFIT	
	New	Renewal	New	Renewal	New	Renewal	New	Renewal	New	Renewal
License Application	X	X	X	X	X	X	X	X	X	X
Worker's Compensation Application	X	X	X	X	X	X	X	X	X	X
INO-Status (Non-US)	X		X		X		X			
Annual Corporate Report				X		X		X		X
Articles & By-Laws (Corporation)			X						X	
Partnership Agreement & Registration					X					
LLC Certificates of Organization Articles of Organization							X			
Sketch of Business Location	X	X	X	X	X	X	X	X	X	X
Original Business License		X		X		X		X		X

Note: Box(es) marked with an **"X"** is a required document that must be submitted with the application.
In addition, **NON-US** Applicant(s) must provide a copy of **PASSPORT** and **ENTRY** or **BUSINESS PERMIT**

SCHEDULE OF FEES:

Banks	$ 500.00	**Manufacturers**	$ 50.00
Offshore Banking	1,300.00	**Wholesalers**	50.00
Security Dealers	300.00		
		Scuba Diving Instruction	$ 100.00
Insurance:		**Scuba Diving Tour Operation**	100.00
Company	$ 300.00		
Broker	100.00		
Agent	75.00	**General Business (per activity)**	$ 50.00
		Roadside Vendors	$ 5.00
Public Utilities	$ 300.00	(Selling Local Agricultural & Fishery Products **ONLY**)	

BUSINESS LICENSE

The latest application may be downloaded at http://cnmidof.net/ where you will also find a complete list of relevant forms and applications.

Business License Application 3 of 3

DIVISION OF REVENUE AND TAXATION
DEPARTMENT OF FINANCE

P.O. Box 5234 CHRB SAIPAN, MP 96950 TEL. (670) 664-1000 FAX. (670) 664-1015

MAP OF BUSINESS LOCATION

(i.e. street name, village, etc)

PHYSICAL LOCATION OF BUSINESS

BUSINESS LICENSE

The latest application may be downloaded at http://cnmidof.net/ where you will also find a complete list of relevant forms and applications.

Saipan, Tinian & Rota Business Offices

Agency or Dept	Mailing Address	Phone/Web Contact
Alco. Bev. & Tobacco Control CNMI Department of Commerce	Caller Box 10007 Capitol Hill, Saipan, MP 96950	Saipan: (670) 664-3026/3065 Fax: (670) 664-3061 Rota: 532-9478; Fax: 532-9510 Tinian: 433-0678; Fax: 433-0853 *www.commerce.gov.mp*
Banking and Insurance Division CNMI Department of Commerce	Caller Box 10007 Capitol Hill, Saipan, MP 96950	Saipan: (670) 664-3008 Fax: (670) 664-3067 Rota: 532-9478; Fax: 532-9510 Tinian: 433-0853; Fax: 433-0678 *Website: www.commerce.gov.mp*
Board of Professional Licensing	P.O. Box 2078 Ascencion Dr #1336 Capitol Hill Saipan, MP 96950	Saipan: (670) 234-4811/4809 Fax: (670) 234-4813
Building Safety Division CNMI Department of Public Works	Caller Box 10007 2nd Floor, Joeten Commercial Building Gualo Rai, Saipan, MP 96950	Saipan: (670) 235-5827/5828 Fax: (670) 235-6346; Rota: 532-3870; Fax: 532-3099; Tinian: 433-9255 Fax: 433-9242 *E-mail: bscadm@netscape.com*
Bureau of Environmental Health Division of Public Health Department of Public Health	P.O. Box 500409 C.K. Navy Hill, Saipan, MP 96950	Saipan: (670) 664-4870/4848/4849 Fax: (670) 664-4871 Rota: 532-9461 Fax: (670) 532-0955 Tinian: 433-0395 Fax: (670) 433-9247
Bureau of Taxicabs Division of Enforcement and Compliance CNMI Department of Commerce	Caller Box 10007 C.K. Capitol Hill, Saipan, MP 96950	Saipan: (670) 664-3014 Fax (670) 664-3093 Rota: 532-9478 Fax: 532-9510 Tinian: 433-0853 Fax: 433-2589
Business Licensing Office, Division of Revenue and Taxation CNMI Department of Finance	P.O. Box 5234 CHRB 2nd Floor, Joeten Commercial Building Dandan, Saipan, MP 96950	Saipan: (670) 664-1000 Fax: (670) 664-1015 Rota: 532-1040/1065 Fax: 532-0473 Tinian: 433-1600 Fax: 433-1615

The telephone area code for Saipan, Tinian and Rota is (670)

Agency or Dept	Mailing Address	Phone/Web Contact
CNMI Bar Association	P.O. Box 504539 Saipan, MP 96950	Saipan: (670) 235-4529 Fax: (670) 235-4528 www.cnmibar.net
CNMI Department of Finance	P.O. Box 5234 CHRB Capitol Hill Saipan, MP 96950	Saipan: (670) 664-1100/01 Fax: (670) 664-1115 Rota: 532-1040; fax: 532-0473 Tinian: 433-1600; fax: 433-1615
CNMI Equal Employment Opportunity Program Office of Personnel Management	P.O. Box 5153 CHRB 2nd Floor, J.M. Building Garapan, Saipan, MP 96950	Saipan:(670)234-6925/6958/ Fax: (670) 234-1013 Rota: 532-9480; fax: 532-9482 Tinian: 433-0032; fax: 433-0031
Central Statistics Division CNMI Department of Commerce	Caller Box 10007 Capitol Hill, Saipan, MP 96950	Saipan: (670) 664-3033 Fax: (670) 664-3066 Rota: 532-9478; fax: 532-9510 Tinian: 433-0853; fax: 433-1054 *www.commerce.gov.mp*
Coastal Resources Management Office Office of the Governor	Caller Box 10007 2nd Floor, Morgen Building San Jose, Saipan, MP 96950	Saipan: (670) 664-8300 Fax: (670) 664-8315 Rota: 532-0464; fax: 532-1000 Tinian: 433-0494; fax: 433-0638 *www.crm.gov.mp*
Commonwealth Development Authority	P.O. Box 502149 Wakin's Building Gualo Rai Saipan, MP 96950	Saipan: (670) 234-6245/6293 Fax: (670) 234-7144/235-7147 Rota: 532-9408; fax: 532-9407 Tinian: 433-9203; fax: 433-3690 *administration@cda.gov.mp* *Website: www.cda.gov.mp*
Commonwealth Utilities Corporation	P.O. Box 501220 Joeten Commercial Bldg Dandan Saipan, MP 96950	Saipan: (670) 235-7025 Fax: (670) 235-6145 Rota: 532-4010; fax: 532-9415 Tinian: 433-9264; fax: 433-9262
Department of the Army Pacific Ocean Division Corps of Engineers Guam Operations Office	Rm 302 San Ramon Bld 115 San Ramon Street Agana, Guam 96910	Saipan: (671) 472-8091

The telephone area code for Saipan, Tinian and Rota is (670)

Agency or Dept	Mailing Address	Phone/Web Contact
Department of Public Lands	P.O. Box 500380 2nd Floor, Joeten Commercial Center Dandan, Saipan, MP 96950	Saipan: (670) 234-3751/3752/3757 Fax: 532-9430 Rota: 532-9431; fax: 234-3755 Tinian: 433-9245; fax: 433-0599
Division of Customs CNMI Department of Finance	P.O. Box 5234 CHRB Puerto Rico, Saipan, MP 96950	Saipan: (670) 664-1601 Fax: (670) 664-1615 Rota: 532-9455; fax: 532-0473 Tinian: 433-1600; fax: 433-1615
Division of Employment Services CNMI Department of Labor	Caller Box 10007 2nd Floor, Afetna Square Building San Antonio, Saipan, MP 96950	Saipan: (670) 236-0926/0928 Fax: (670) 236-0994 Rota: 532-9448; fax: 532-9468 Tinian: 433-3707; fax: 433-3730
Division of Environmental Quality	P.O. Box 501304 Gualo Rai Commercial Center Gualo Rai, Saipan, MP 96950	Tel: (670) 664-8500 Fax: (670) 664-8540 Rota: 532-3102; Fax: 532-3103 Tinian: 433-3169; fax: 433-3169 *E-mail: deq@saipan.com*
Division of Fish and Wildlife Department of Lands and Natural Resources	P.O. Box 10007 Lower Base, Saipan, MP 96950	Saipan: (670) 664-6000 Fax: (670) 664-6060 Rota: 532-6000; fax: 532-0520 Tinian: 433-9298 fax: 433-3152
Division of Historic Preservation Department of Community and Cultural Affairs	Saipan, MP 96950	Saipan: (670) 664-2120 Fax: (670) 664-2139 Rota: 532-0818; fax: 532-0818 Tinian: 433-0220; fax: 433-0220
Division of Immigration Office of the Attorney General	Caller Box 10007 2nd Floor, Afetna Square Building San Antonio, Saipan, MP 96950	Saipan: (670) 664-0920 Fax: (670) 664-3190 Rota: 532-9436 Tinian: 433-3712; fax: 433-3730
Division of Labor CNMI Department of Labor	Caller Box 10007 2nd Floor, Afetna Square Building San Antonio, Saipan, MP 96950	Saipan: (670) 236-0900/0907 Fax: (670) 236-0991 Rota: 532-9429; fax: 532-9468; Tinian: 433-3700; fax: 433-3730

The telephone area code for Saipan, Tinian and Rota is (670)

Agency or Dept	Mailing Address	Phone/Web Contact
Division of Revenue and Taxation CNMI Department of Finance	P.O. Box 5234 CHRB 1st Floor, Joeten Commercial Building Dandan, Saipan, MP 96950	Saipan: (670) 664-1000 Fax: (670) 664-1015 Rota: 532-1040; fax: 532-0473 Tinian: 433-1600; fax: 433-1615
Foreign Investment Office CNMI Department of Commerce	Caller Box 10007 Capitol Hill, Saipan, MP 96950	Saipan: (670) 664-3017/8 Fax: (670) 664-3067 Rota: 532-9478; Fax: 532-9510 Tinian: 433-0853; Fax:433-0678
Hotel Association of the Northern Mariana Islands	P.O. Box 5075 CHRB Saipan, MP 96950	Saipan: (670) 233-1420 Fax: (670) 233-1424 www.marianashotels.org
Marianas Visitors Authority	P.O. Box 500861 CK Saipan, MP 96950	Saipan: (670) 664-3200 Fax: (670) 664-3237 Rota: 532-0327; fax: 532-4000 Tinian: 433-9365; fax: 433-0653 *E-mail: mva@saipan.com* *Website: www.mymarianas.com*
Occupational Safety and Health Administration Saipan Office U.S. Department of Labor		Saipan: (670) 323-1201/322-3758
Registrar of Corporations CNMI Department of Commerce	Caller Box 10007 2nd Floor, Joeten Commercial Building, Room 27 Dandan, Saipan, MP 96950	Saipan: (670) 664-3002 Fax: (670) 664-1015
Saipan Chamber of Commerce	P.O. Box 500806 1st Floor, Family Building Garapan, Saipan, MP 96950	Saipan: (670) 235-7699 Fax: (670) 233-7151 *Email:saipanchamber@saipan.com* *Website: www.saipanchamber.com*

The telephone area code for Saipan, Tinian and Rota is (670)

Agency or Dept	Mailing Address	Phone/Web Contact
Small Business Development Ctr Northern Marianas College	P.O. Box 501250 C.K. As Terlaje Campus, Building T As Terlaje, Saipan, MP 96950	Saipan: (670) 235-1551/1552 Fax: (670) 235-5383
Social Security Administration	2nd Floor, Marina Heights II Building Puerto Rico Saipan, MP 96950	Saipan: (670) 234-6683 Fax: (670) 234-3022 Rota: (670) 532-9421 Tinian: (670) 433-9421 *www.ssa.gov/employer*
Tinian Casino Gaming Control Commission	P.O. Box 143 Tinian, MP 96952	Saipan: (670) 433-0063 Fax: (670) 433-9290 *contact@tiniangamingcommission.com www.tiniangamingcommission.com*
Workers' Compensation Commission NMI Retirement Fund	P.O. Box 501247 2nd Floor, NMI Retirement Fund Bldg Capitol Hill Saipan, MP 96950	Saipan: (670) 664-8024 Fax: (670) 664-8074 Rota: 532-9516; fax: 532-9486 Tinian: 433-3733; fax: 433-3863

The telephone area code for Saipan, Tinian and Rota is (670)

Saipan Facts from CIA.gov

Saipan Geography

Location:	Oceania, islands in the North Pacific Ocean, about three-quarters of the way from Hawaii to the Philippines
Geographic coordinates:	15 12 N, 145 45 E
Area:	*total:* 477 sq km *land:* 477 sq km *note:* includes 14 islands including Saipan, Rota, and Tinian
Area - US comparative:	2.5 times the size of Washington, DC* (see footnote below)
Coastline:	1,482 km
Maritime claims:	*territorial sea:* 12 nm *exclusive economic zone:* 200 nm
Climate:	tropical marine; moderated by northeast trade winds, little seasonal temperature variation; dry season December to June, rainy season July to October
Terrain:	southern islands are limestone with level terraces and fringing coral reefs; northern islands are volcanic
Elevation extremes:	Mt. Tapochau on Saipan at 1,554 feet is the highest point. The measurement from the floor of the Marianas Trench to the crest of Mount Tapochau is 37,752 feet or 7.15 statute miles, (from sea level Mount Everest measures 29,028 feet). Saipan's 54 mile coastline
Natural resources:	arable land, fish
Land use:	*arable land:* 13.04% *permanent crops:* 4.35% *other:* 82.61% (2005)
Natural hazards:	active volcanoes on Pagan and Agrihan; typhoons (especially August to November)
Environment - current issues:	contamination of groundwater on Saipan may contribute to disease; clean-up of landfill; protection of endangered species conflicts with development

** As an interesting comparison for international readers, Saipan's total land area is 120 sq km or 46.5 square miles. To put that in perspective*
- Saipan is about the size of San Francisco.
- Saipan is slightly larger than Hong Kong but smaller than the District of Columbia.
- Saipan is smaller than Barbados (CNMI's 14 islands equal Barbados)
- Manhattan is 59.5 sq km (23 sq mi) = Saipan is exactly twice the size of Manhattan
- Staten Island encompasses 151.5 sq km (58.5 sq mi) a little larger than Saipan
- The Bronx is 109 sq km (42 sq mi) a little smaller than Saipan
- Queens is 282.9 sq km (109.2 sq mi) a bit more than twice the size of Saipan
- Brooklyn is 182.9 sq km (70.6 sq mi) just 1.5 times the size of Saipan
Brooklyn has 2.5 million people compared to the 60,000 or so who live on Saipan
- Jamaica's land area is 4,411 square miles

For additional information, visit http://www.cnmi-guide.com/info/main.html
http://www.odci.gov/cia/publications/factbook_old/print/cq.html

Saipan People

Population:	86,616 (July 2008 est.)
Age structure:	*0-14 years:* 18.4% (male 8,342/female 7,594) *15-64 years:* 79.9% (male 27,996/female 41,245) *65 years and over:* 1.7% (male 740/female 699) (2008 est.)
Median age:	*total:* 29.9 years *male:* 32 years *female:* 28.9 years (2008 est.)
Population growth rate:	2.377% (2008 est.)
Birth rate:	19.04 births/1,000 population (2008 est.)
Death rate:	2.31 deaths/1,000 population (2008 est.)
Net migration rate:	7.04 migrant(s)/1,000 population (2008 est.)
Sex ratio:	*at birth:* 1.06 male(s)/female *under 15 years:* 1.1 male(s)/female *15-64 years:* 0.68 male(s)/female *65 years and over:* 1.06 male(s)/female *total population:* 0.75 male(s)/female (2008 est.)
Infant mortality rate:	*total:* 6.72 deaths/1,000 live births *male:* 6.68 deaths/1,000 live births *female:* 6.76 deaths/1,000 live births (2008 est.)
Life expectancy at birth:	*total population:* 76.5 years *male:* 73.89 years *female:* 79.26 years (2008 est.)
Total fertility rate:	1.18 children born/woman (2008 est.)
Nationality:	*noun:* NA (US citizens) *adjective:* NA
Ethnic groups:	Asian 56.3%, Pacific islander 36.3%, Caucasian 1.8%, other 0.8%, mixed 4.8% (2000 census)
Religions:	Christian (Roman Catholic majority, although traditional beliefs and taboos may still be found)
Languages:	Philippine languages 24.4%, Chinese 23.4%, Chamorro 22.4%, English 10.8%, other Pacific island languages 9.5%, other 9.6% (2000 census)
Literacy:	*definition:* age 15 and over can read and write *total population:* 97% *male:* 97% *female:* 96% (1980 est.)

Many of the statistics for "The People" are based on the local/indigenous population and US Citizens. Please note that Saipan has many different nationalities and populations each with their own distinct statistics.

Saipan Government

Country name: *conventional long form:* Commonwealth of the Northern Mariana Islands
conventional short form: Northern Mariana Islands
abbreviation: CNMI
former: Trust Territory of the Pacific Islands, Mariana Islands

Dependency status: commonwealth in political union with the US; federal funds to the Commonwealth administered by the US Department of the Interior, Office of Insular Affairs

Government type: commonwealth; self-governing with locally elected governor, lieutenant governor, and legislature

Capital: *name:* Saipan
geographic coordinates: 15 12 N, 145 45 E
time difference: UTC+10 (15 hours ahead of Washington, DC during Standard Time)

Administrativ e divisions: none (commonwealth in political union with the US); there are no first-order administrative divisions as defined by the US Government, but there are four municipalities at the second order: Northern Islands, Rota, Saipan, Tinian

Independence : none (commonwealth in political union with the US)

National holiday: Commonwealth Day, 8 January (1978)

Constitution: Constitution of the Commonwealth of the Northern Mariana Islands effective 1 January 1978; Covenant Agreement fully effective 4 November 1986

Legal system: based on US system, except for customs, wages, immigration laws, and taxation

Suffrage: 18 years of age; universal; indigenous inhabitants are US citizens but do not vote in US presidential elections

Executive branch: *chief of state:* President Barak Obama of the US (since 20 January 2001); Vice President Joseph Biden (since January 2009)
head of government: Governor Benigno R. FITIAL (since 9 January 2006); Lieutenant Governor Timothy P. VILLAGOMEZ (since 9 January 2006)
cabinet: the cabinet consists of the heads of the 10 principal departments under the executive branch who are appointed by the governor with the advice and consent of the Senate; other members include Special Assistants to the governor and office heads appointed by and reporting directly to the governor
elections: under the US Constitution, residents of unincorporated territories, such as the Commonwealth of the Northern Mariana Islands, do not vote in elections for US president and vice president; however, they may vote in the Democratic and Republican presidential primary elections; governor and lieutenant governor elected on the same ticket by popular vote for four-year terms (eligible for a second term); election last held 5 November 2005 (next to be held in November 2009)
election results: Benigno R. FITIAL elected governor in a four-way race; percent of vote - Benigno R. FITIAL 28.07%, Heinz HOFSCHNEIDER 27.34%, Juan BABAUTA 26.6%, Froilan TENORIO 17.99%

Saipan Government, continued

Legislative branch: bicameral Legislature consists of the Senate (9 seats; members are elected by popular vote to serve four-year staggered terms) and the House of Representatives (20 seats; members are elected by popular vote to serve two-year terms)
elections: Senate - last held 3 November 2007 (next to be held in November 2009); House of Representatives - last held 3 November 2007 (next to be held in November 2009)
election results: Senate - percent of vote by party - NA; seats by party - Covenant Party 3, Republican Party 3, Democratic Party 1, independents 2; House of Representatives - percent of vote by party - NA; seats by party - Republican Party 12, Covenant Party 4, Democratic Party 1, independents 3
note: the Northern Mariana Islands does not have a nonvoting delegate in the US Congress; instead, it has an elected official or "resident representative" in Washington, DC; seats by party - Republican Party 1 (Pedro A. TENORIO)

Judicial branch: Commonwealth Supreme Court; Superior Court; Federal District Court

Political parties and leaders: Covenant Party [Benigno R. FITIAL]; Democratic Party [Dr. Carlos S. CAMACHO]; Republican Party [Juan S. REYES]

Political pressure groups and leaders: NA

International organization participation: Interpol (subbureau), SPC, UPU

Flag description: blue, with a white, five-pointed star superimposed on the gray silhouette of a latte stone (a traditional foundation stone used in building) in the center, surrounded by a wreath

Saipan Economy

Economy - overview:	The economy benefits substantially from financial assistance from the US. The rate of funding has declined as locally generated government revenues have grown. The key tourist industry employs about 50% of the work force and accounts for roughly one-fourth of GDP. Japanese tourists predominate. The agricultural sector is made up of cattle ranches and small farms producing coconuts, breadfruit, tomatoes, and melons.
GDP (purchasing power parity):	$900 million *note:* GDP estimate includes US subsidy (2000 est.)
GDP (exchange rate):	$633.4 million (2000)
GDP - per capita (PPP):	$12,500 (2000 est.)
GDP - composition by sector:	*agriculture:* NA% *industry:* NA% *services:* NA%
Labor force:	44,470 total indigenous labor force; 2,699 unemployed; 28,717 foreign workers (2000)
Labor force - by occupation:	*agriculture:* NA% *industry:* NA% *services:* NA%
Unemployment rate:	3.9% (2001)
Population below poverty line:	NA%
Household income or consumption by percentage share:	*lowest 10%:* NA% *highest 10%:* NA%
Inflation rate (consumer prices):	-0.8% (2000)
Budget:	*revenues:* $193 million *expenditures:* $223 million (FY01/02 est.)
Agriculture - products:	coconuts, fruits, vegetables; cattle
Industries:	tourism, construction, garments, handicrafts
Industrial production growth rate:	NA%
Electricity - production:	NA kWh
Electricity - consumption:	NA kWh
Electricity - exports:	0 kWh (2007 est.)
Electricity - imports:	0 kWh (2007 est.)
Exports:	$NA
Exports - partners:	US (2006)
Imports:	$214.4 million (2001)
Imports - commodities:	food, construction equipment and materials, petroleum products
Imports - partners:	US, Japan (2006)
Economic aid - recipient:	extensive funding from US
Debt - external:	$NA
Currency:	US dollar (USD)
Exchange rates:	the US dollar is used
Fiscal year:	1 October - 30 September

Saipan Communications System

Telephones - main lines in use:	21,000 (2000)
Telephones - mobile cellular:	20,500 (2004)
Telephone system:	*general assessment:* NA *domestic:* NA *international:* country code - 1-670; satellite earth stations - 2 Intelsat (Pacific Ocean)
Radio broadcast stations:	AM 1, FM 6, shortwave 1 (2005)
Television broadcast stations:	1 (on Saipan; in addition, 2 cable services on Saipan provide varied programming from satellite networks) (2006)
Internet country code:	.mp
Internet hosts:	5 (2007)
Internet users:	10,000 (2003)

The Transportation System

Airports:	5 (2007)
Airports - with paved runways:	*total:* 3 *2,438 to 3,047 m:* 2 *1,524 to 2,437 m:* 1 (2007)
Airports - with unpaved runways:	*total:* 2 *2,438 to 3,047 m:* 1 *under 914 m:* 1 (2007)
Heliports:	1 (2007)
Roadways:	*total:* 536 km (2004)
Ports and terminals:	Saipan, Tinian

The Military

Military - note:	defense is the responsibility of the US

Transnational Issues

Disputes - international:	none

GLOSSARY

Alcoholic beverage: beer or other malt beverage, distilled alcoholic beverage, wine or sake and any other beverage which contains at least one-half of one percent (.5%) of alcohol by volume and which is fit for human consumption.

arable: specifically, land capable of being farmed productively

Carolinian: The Carolinian, or Refaluwasch, people are an Austronesian ethnic group who originated in the South Pacific, eastern Caroline Islands, with a total population of around 8,500 people. It is thought that their ancestors may have originally immigrated from Asia and Indonesia to Micronesia around 2,000 years ago.

Chamorro: The Chamorro/Chamoru people are the indigenous people of the Mariana Islands, which include the American territory of Guam and the United States Commonwealth of the Northern Mariana Islands in Micronesia.

CNMI: Commonwealth of the Northern Mariana Islands. a 14-island archipelago which includes the 3 inhabited islands of Saipan, Tinian and Rota

C.K. Chalan Kanoa, a village on Saipan.

Consumer goods: products, goods & materials including but not limited to vehicles, retail products, garment material, construction material and all goods that have any form of packaging.

CNMI Covenant: *The Covenant to Establish a Commonwealth of the Northern Mariana Islands in Political Union with the United States of America* defines the unique relationship between the Northern Mariana Islands and the United States, recognizing U.S. sovereignty but limiting, in some respects, applicability of federal law. View http://cnmilaw.org/covenant.htm

Cold War: a conflict over ideological differences carried on by methods short of sustained overt military action and usually without breaking off diplomatic relations; the ideological conflict between the United States and the Union of Soviet Socialist Republics (Russia) during later part of the 20th century.

Earhart, Amelia: first woman aviator to fly solo nonstop across the Atlantic (1928); while attempting to fly around the world she disappeared over the Pacific (1898-1937)

expat: short for expatriate; a person who is temporarily or permanently residing in a country and culture other than that of the person's upbringing or legal residence. The word comes from the Latin ex (out of) and patria (country, fatherland).

Federalization: The enforcement of the CNMI's labor laws and the change in immigration laws and enforcement federal standards.

Free Trade Zone: popularly known as FTZ, is an area where goods may be traded without any barriers imposed by customs authorities like quotas and tariffs. (FTZ) is a special designated area within a country where normal trade barriers like quotas, tariffs are removed and the bureaucratic necessities are narrowed in order to attract new business and foreign investments.

IR: Immediate Relatives. Includes spouses, children, but does not include other relatives.

manifesto: A public declaration of principles, policies, or intentions, especially of a political nature.

Marianas Trench: Marine trench in the floor of the western North Pacific Ocean. It is the deepest known depression on the surface of the Earth, with a maximum depth of 36,201 ft (11,034 m). The trench extends from southeast of Guam to northwest of the Mariana Islands, a distance of more than 1,580 mi (2,550 km), and has a mean width of 43 mi (69 km).

Northern Islands: the CNMI is comprised of fourteen islands. The three inhabited southern islands are Saipan, Tinian and Rota. The other 10 islands, referred to as the "northern islands" are either uninhabited or sparsely inhabited.

pandemic: An epidemic (a sudden outbreak) of an illness like the flu, that becomes very widespread and affects a whole region, a continent, or the world.

passionpreneur: a term coined by Walt Goodridge which refers to someone who has used a passion, talent/hobby as the basis of an entrepreneurial venture.

PAWS: Pet Assistance Welfare Service.

probate: The process of legally establishing the validity of a will before a judicial authority

soft drink: any readily drinkable carbonated or non-carbonated non-alcoholic beverage, other than drinkable dairy products, one hundred percent fruit or veg juices, bottled drinking water.

touwlawos: "Those of us who live and work on Saipan"

user fees: government tax imposed on business revenues. The customs user fee was one such tax imposed on exports by the now defunct garment industry which resulted in 80 million dollars annually flowing to the CNMI government.

vegan: vegetarian who shuns eating, drinking or using any products derived from animals.

Visa Waiver Program: This refers to a specific section of Immigration law Public Law 110-229

Research & Bibliography

☐ Setting up Business in the CNMI: A Guide for Investors
Commonwealth Development Authority (2006)

Further Reading

☐ *The New Saipan Agenda available for free download (www.newsaipan.com)*

☐ *Chicken Feathers and Garlic Skin: Diary of a Chinese Factory Girl on Saipan* by Chun Yu Wang as told to Walt F.J. Goodridge *(www.saipanfactorygirl.com)*

☐ Public Law 110.229 Regarding the Federalization of Immigration
Public laws may be found archived at
Northern Marianas Commonwealth Legislature website at
http://www.cnmileg.gov.mp/

☐ For an informative online resource as well as essays by economist William Stewart, visit www.cnmi-guide.com/info

☐ *Saipan Atlas*
Order at SaipanLiving.com

☐ Covenant to Establish a Commonwealth of the Northern Mariana Islands in Political Union with the United States of America
View a copy at: www.cnmilaw.org/covenant.htm

☐ To keep up to date with Immigration on Saipan visit the Department of Homeland Security website
www.dhs.gov

Websites

- *www.SaipanLiving.com*

- *www.BestofSaipan.com*

- *www.DestinationSaipan.com*

More!

The SaipanLiving™ Survival Series of Guides
presented by SaipanLiving.com

Doing Business On Saipan
A step-by-step survival guide for finding opportunity, launching a business and profiting in the US Commonwealth of the Northern Mariana Islands of Saipan, Tinian and Rota

The Saipan Consumer Guide
Reviews of businesses on Saipan, Tinian & Rota

The Saipan Immigration Report
Everything you need to know about status of visitors, tourists, residents, citizens and their immediate relatives living in the Northern Mariana Islands.

Order all three and save!
Details at Saipanliving.com!

About the Author

Walt F.J. Goodridge is a Columbia University graduate, former civil engineer, author and entrepreneur who, in 2006, "discovered" Saipan, booked a one-way ticket, and escaped from New York to live our his nomadpreneur dream on this pacific island paradise.

Once here, and wanting to be a part of the re-branding of Saipan's image, he conceived of and launched the WeLoveSaipan.com website, Saipanliving.com, and 20 additional sites devoted to showing the world the often overlooked images and impressions of Saipan, CNMI (Commonwealth of the Northern Mariana Islands). [See BestofSaipan.com for links to all of Walt's sites.]

Walt writes a weekly business column for the Saipan Tribune entitled " The Saipanpreneur Project." He has written *Doing Business on Saipan* to further encourage entrepreneurial activity and investment on the island. with former garment factory worker Chun Yu Wang, Walt co-authored *Chicken Feathers and Garlic Skin: Diary of a Chinese Garment Factory Girl on Saipan*. He is the founder of Destination Saipan Marketing, Inc, and was recently recognized by official CNMI Senate Resolution No. 15-54 for his invaluable contributions to Saipan, its residents and economy.

Walt currently owns and operates over 50 websites, has written a total of 16 books, over 400 business and motivational articles and almost 500 inspiration poems.

Walt is originally from the island of Jamaica. You can read about his first year and impressions of Saipan in the book *Jamaican on Saipan!*

Contact Walt at P.O. Box 503991, Saipan, MP 96950, or via email at Walt@saipanliving.com.

Saipan on DVD!

Check out these DVDs for more about Saipan, it's people, culture and beauty, created by Saipanpreneurs here on island!

Lieweila: A Micronesian Story: Narrated by Cinta Kaipat, a descendant of the first migrants, the film tells the history of the Refalawasch people beginning with details of the early migrations and ending with their current situation on Saipan. *($27.00)*

State of Liberty: Looking for America, is the pilot episode of a series which captures life, love and the pursuit of happiness here on Saipan. Filmmaker Dan Shor states: *"it's a story about the microcosm of the world that populates this tiny little island. Our lead characters are Japanese, Chinese, Chamorro, Carolinian, Bangladeshi, Filipino, Russian, and stateside Americans."* Everyone is represented, even the Jamaican(s) on the island.

The Underwater World of Saipan is a 105-minute DVD showcasing the incredible beauty and bio-diversity of Saipan's underwater world. This DVD takes you on 7 distinctly different dives including The Grotto, Obyan, Banzai Cliff, Ice Cream, Managaha, Naftan Point and Lau Lau Bay. by Mike Tripp *($25.00)*

Order these and other unique gifts at
www.saipanliving.com

Saipan in paperback

Chicken Feathers and Garlic Skin:

Diary of a Chinese Garment Factory Girl on Saipan by Chun Yu Wang, as told to Walt Goodridge

This groundbreaking book is the only account of what life was like for the thousands of garment factory workers who lived on Saipian between the Garment Factory era of 1984 to 2009.

Back Cover: It took a lot of courage for a 25-year-old girl from Wu Xi City in Jiang Shu province, China, who had never flown on a plane, and who had never left home before, to travel 2,000 miles to a foreign country in search of work. It took even more courage to stay once she discovered.......(www.saipanfactorygirl.com)

ISBN: 9780974531342; $14.95

Jamaican on Saipan!

Walt F.J. Goodridge

(author of *Turn Your Passion Into Profit* and *Doing Business on Saipan*

Enjoy this light-hearted account of Walt's escape from America to live his nomadpreneur dream on the island of Saipan. step-by-step guide for finding opportunity, launching by

ISBN: 9780974531359; $19.95

Doing Business on *Saipan!*

A step-by-step guide for finding opportunity, launching a business and profiting in the US Commonwealth of the Northern Mariana Islands

by Walt F.J. Goodridge

(author of *Turn Your Passion Into Profit*)

ISBN: 9780974531359; $19.95

Order these and other products at
www.saipanliving.com

Other Products by Walt F.J. Goodridge

(most are available in ebook,and paperback formats)

Turn Your Passion Into Profit (ebook, paperback, 6-CD)
The Tao of Wow
The Ageless Adept
Change the Game
Hip Hop Entrepreneur Lists of Exposure
This Game of Hip Hop Artist Management
Life Rhymes for the Passion-Centered Life
Come into Our Whirl
Lessons in Success
Hip Hop Profits
The Hip Hop Record Label Business Plan
The Niche Market Report
Chicken Feathers and Garlic Skin
Jamaican on Saipan
Doing Business on Saipan
Living True to Your Self

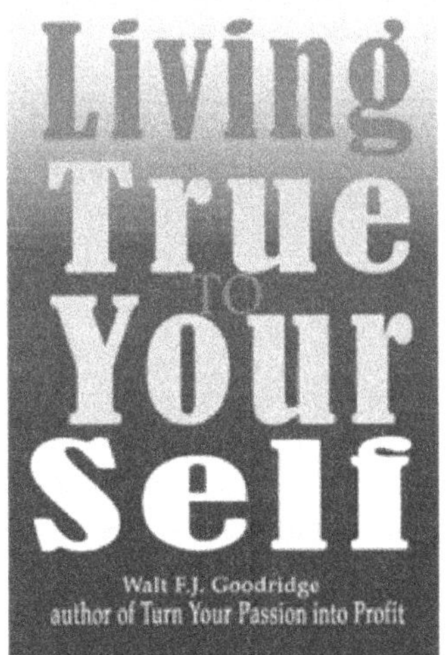

Creating the Life You've Always Dreamed of
by Walt F.J. Goodridge
(author of *Turn Your Passion Into Profit*)
Living true to your self requires that you adopt a new belief system about yourself, others, and the world you live in. It requires that you identify what's true, find your purpose, develop an effective survival strategy, overcome inertia, motivate your self consistently, sustain momentum, decipher the Universe's code to recognize the opportunities and harness the power in the setbacks, evolve in the direction of life's clues, while honoring body, mind and spirit...and that's just for starters! Who better to guide you through the internal dialogue, thoughts, and actions that can make it possible for you than Walt Goodridge, passion coach, nomadpreneur, and author of 16 books, who escaped the rat race to live his personal dream on a Pacific Island?
Visit www.passionprofit.com/livingtrue ;$19.95

a complete product list, along with articles, free reports and a passion personality test are available at www.passionprofit.com